Katie Sutherland is a freelance journalist, published in a wide range of Australian newspapers and magazines. She is a regular contributor to *The Conversation*, primarily writing about cultural representations of autism. Katie holds a Doctorate of Creative Arts and when she's not writing, she works as a tutor and researcher at Western Sydney University. She lives in Sydney with her husband, two teenage boys and a rambunctious dog. *Temples and Towers: Everyday stories of families living with autism* is her first book.

Temples and Towers: Everyday stories of families living with autism

Katie Sutherland

First published by Katie Sutherland in 2020
This edition published in 2020 by Katie Sutherland

Temples and Towers: Everyday stories of families living with autism

EPUB: 9781922389473
POD: 9781922389480

Cover design by Red Tally Studios

Publishing services provided by Critical Mass
www.critmassconsulting.com

For my two boys, whom I love immeasurably

'*There is a crack in everything, that's how the light gets in.*'
Leonard Cohen, *Anthem*, 1994

'*I would say that we autistics are just coming into our time.*'
John Elder Robison, *All in the mind*,
ABC Radio, 2016

Contents

Introduction

'In exposure we can influence what is "normal" and people then cease to see or recognise the "difference".'
Andrew Solomon, Sydney Writer's Festival, 2014.

I am clutching my large belly and listening to Elton John sing *Rocket Man*. Tom's in-utero name was Rocket and my husband James and I decided this to be his theme song. Little did we know how fitting the moniker actually was—that in moments, our mini space explorer would catch us by surprise and jet-propel himself into the universe in a speedy, no-fuss delivery, two weeks early. Nor did we have any sense of just how much he would continue to amaze and challenge us.

We were expecting friends for dinner and the house was the cleanest it had been for months. I'd finally finished a stressful job as a public relations consultant just two days prior and I was looking forward to celebrating. The dinner party, however, was never to be.

I pictured myself having a water birth, but tried not to get my hopes up, because I'd heard how birth plans could come unraveled. As it turns out, you don't need a written document for plans to go awry. I intended having my baby in the hospital's birth centre, which is supported by midwives. But upon arrival, my contractions in full swing, we discovered the doors to the birth centre were closed. Locked shut, in fact. The midwives were on their dinner break, so I was ushered into a sparse-looking observation room. There were no essential oils burning, no ambient music playing. I wasn't even offered pain killers so quick was the process. Such was my welcome to the world of parenting and my first lesson in relinquishing all control. At 8.30pm, after just three hours in labour, I rang our dinner guests and told them that the beef ragu would have to wait. The Rocket had been launched and we were the shocked parents of a beautiful, new baby boy.

From the moment of his birth, Tom has continued to teach me about the importance of managing expectations. He still surprises me in ways I would never have imagined. Who knew, for example, that this baby would be born with such innate creativity and would grow to become such a wonderful artist? Or that he would develop such a strong sense of social justice? Raising a child with autism has also taught me many things about myself. I'd like to think I am less judgmental and that I don't jump to conclusions about people quite so quickly now, or at least, I catch myself out when I do. Where once I might have thought a person rude for not looking at me in the eye, I now realise they may have a reason (eye contact can be confronting for some autistic individuals). I am also much more aware that so much of what we consider 'normal', stems from societal expectation. In countries, such as China and Japan, looking a person directly in the eye can be considered disrespectful, yet in Western cultures, we are taught not to trust people who avoid eye contact. The 'social model of disability' hinges on such cultural judgments. It is a theoretical framework that focusses on how disability is perceived, rather than the actual impairment and describes disability as a "social, cultural and historically specific phenomenon".[1] Within this model, discrimination is a derivative of deep-seated beliefs and stigma, rather than innate attributes.

I have spent a great deal of time trying to understand how discrimination is made and how it affects my child and family. How culture creates ideas and how these ideas translate into attitudes and actions, positive, neutral and negative. Much of this investigation has been through examining my own lived experience. However, I have also chosen to consciously engage with the expertise of others who live with autism, in one way or another, and to delve into theory. This combination has helped me to make sense of both Tom's experience of autism and the ways society views autistic individuals. In this process of engaging with both the public and private spheres, I have come to the conclusion that we are all part of a human continuum and, as Susan Sontag writes, that illness or disability will eventually effect all of us in some way.[2] Autism is a part of some people and I believe we would all be better off if, rather than problematising, stigmatising and fearing it, we viewed it as an important component of the human experience. Potentially, a boon rather than a burden. If we are to flourish, we have a collective responsibility to ensure everyone is provided with equal opportunities, including education and employment. And that starts with one word; compassion.

When Tom was little he used to spend hours drawing with pencils and crayons. He would escape into the worlds he created, lofty skyscrapers and the cityscapes of Manhattan or Sydney and intricate imaginary places of mountains, rivers and forests. He would emerge from his drawing sessions with hair ruffled, crayon under his fingernails and smudges on his cheeks. I remember once extracting pieces of paper from him while trying to clear the table for dinner and discovering beautiful crayon depictions of Uluru, each one replicating the picture before it, but with a different colour scheme of the rock at dusk; red, orange, purple and green. I still have the pictures archived in the cupboard along with piles of others, and plan to one day have them framed.[3]

Tom found drawing relaxing as a little kid, and still does. As an adolescent, he continues to draw prolifically both at home and at school (much to his maths and science teachers' chagrin). He won a competition for a pencil drawing of our dog and for a while, he ran a side business doing commissions of people's pets. As well as drawing, he loves computer games and exploring the world on Google Earth. He aspires to be a designer or 'something architecture-related', having once boasted that he was going to build the tallest building in the world. We used to tell him to aim high and reach for the sky. We didn't think he'd take us literally.

Tom is a sweet, creative, funny person with many talents. Although, of course, if it was that simple and I was that accepting, I wouldn't be here, now, writing this book. While Tom's social skills have really progressed, he can still find some social settings overwhelming and sometimes still experiences crippling anxiety. Tom has learning differences and his challenges are complex. These challenges have been revealed over time and across his developmental stages. While each revelation has had its own challenges, this gradual process has allowed James and I to put the puzzle pieces together over time. For example, discovering just why Tom finds the classroom such a tricky place to learn. He has consistently struggled in a public school system that, quite frankly, is underfunded and ill-equipped to cater for the many atypical children that face similar challenges every day. This is; of course, despite a number of good teachers who have their students' best interests in mind and work with the resources they have.[4] Tom's struggles have changed over time, each requiring the development of a different set of skills for him, for us and for the education system. This has required a degree of advocacy from us as parents that we were ill-equipped for in the beginning, as well as courage, persistence, humour and the long slog so familiar to all parents of differently-abled young people.

Our diverse ideas around autism are mirrored in the way our children accept their conditions. When Tom's little brother Otis was in Year One he proudly told his teacher "my brother is so Asperger's with countries and cultures" when the class was studying geography. What he meant was that his brother was a whiz with geography and spent a lot of time recalling information from atlases. I was heartened when a teacher friend recently told me about a 13-year-old student at a mainstream school who, after blitzing his maths exam, announced to the class "that's my autistic genius coming out." His parents had been open with him about his autism from an early age and he felt no need to hide his strengths to his peers. Juxtaposing this are some parents who choose not to discuss autism with their children for fear it may harm them if they are categorised as 'different' to other children. While I empathise with the need to protect your child however you can, it saddens me that we continue to speak in whispers about autism. It can send a message to children that it is something to be ashamed of. We should celebrate diversity and difference. In the words of author and comedian Kathy Lette, talking about her adult son with autism, "Difference is good."

Autistic artist Dawn-joy Leong also believes that diversity is important, and that autism is not the barren landscape that many people understand it to be. She says the autistic mind is "a thriving ecology teeming with abundant detail, nuances, texture, tastes, sounds, images, smells, profound thought and imagination". Autistic artists, she believes, have much to offer the neurotypical world and I agree.[5] In my research I have found that many neurodiverse people have a sensory connection with the world that neurotypicals lack—appreciating the beauty or detail in what others might consider mundane.[6] In the arts, for instance, this can represent the colours of a painting, the tone of a music note or the empathic resonance of a poem. If creativity is essentially a matter of thinking differently, then surely the world needs autistic people, not just in the creative arts, but also in the realms of business and technology.

Speaking with autistic individuals and their families has helped me to appreciate the beauty of being differently wired. It has enabled me to see a little of the 'thriving ecology' that provides so much wisdom, insight and joy to those who swim against the tide. It has also enabled me to see the persistence and resilience necessary to survive, being outside the slipstream. Despite increased awareness of autism, discrimination, stigma and misunderstanding remain commonplace. While there are growing numbers of employers who can see the benefits of employing neurodiverse workers, and schools and universities are working to be more inclusive, it remains the case that autistic people still find getting a job more difficult, require greater support in education and are routinely stereotyped in the media and in the mainstream. As disability employment consultant, Martin Wren, told me, "We all want to be accepting. But the fact of the matter is that the vast majority of people have a bandwidth of conformity that they expect everybody to be in." The reality is that attitudes towards diversity are still evolving. If job seekers want paid employment they may need some guidance in how to navigate a neurotypical world.[7] Without support, they may suffer from social isolation and lack of connection or belonging, struggling to receive the respect and dignity necessary to thrive.

The interviews for this book have been enormously rewarding and those interviewed have contributed with great generosity not just to this book, but also to society as a whole. Their stories of adversity, have no doubt contributed to their resilience, for theirs are not safe and familiar narratives, of perfection or 'normality'. They are stories of chaos and ambiguity, valid and authentic, demonstrating in detail, in beauty and in action, why diversity matters.

The people you will meet include Anna and George and their daughter Cassie, who loves writing fan fiction and growing plants from seed. Anna is a pioneer, in that her two daughters were diagnosed in the 1990s before many people knew what Asperger's was. Her path has not been an easy one, but her tenacity has enabled her and her children to thrive despite systemic and personal obstacles. I also write about Catherine, a preschool teacher, and her son Louis who wants to study volcanology at university, and about Juliet and her son Gabriel. Juliet is a Latina-Australian artist who transformed the garden of her son's school to create a tranquil sensory oasis where he and other children could relax. Then there is the story of Sylvia and her son Alex, whose family grow tomatoes to sell at the markets each weekend. Alex's sense of smell was once so strong that he could not sit at the family table to eat meals—but he now draws on his powerful senses to craft recipes that marry together unusual herbs and ingredients. "In life we must accept ourselves for who and what we are," muses a philosophical Alex. "That is the road to happiness. The key is knowing who you are. Life is all about discovering yourself." We meet Liesel, who rose above her traumatic school years to become an opera singer living in Europe. Liesel's mother Susan has five adult children on the spectrum. "A lot of parents think it's the worst thing that ever happened to me, but in actual fact it's not," says Susan. "I just love their individuality and creativity." And I introduce you to Zac and his mother Jacinta, who, after years of struggling with Zac's erratic behavior, has found solace, understanding and strategies in his diagnosis.

I often found myself overwhelmed with emotion in the interviews. As a journalist this surprised me and I wondered if, in talking to other parents and listening to their children, I had been understood myself—if through the sharing of stories we have built a community, a place to rest and to think. It is my hope that I can now 'pay forward' this sense of kinship with an even broader audience, particularly to parents who may be feeling afraid or isolated.

Through sharing these stories, I hope to contribute to a "circle of shared experience" as sociologist Arthur Frank calls it—to offer companionship to those who might need it and subsequently contribute to a broader dialogue around autism. For, as tempting as it is to stay quiet, there is still too much that needs to be addressed to remain silent. While I know that this book does not cover all possible issues or represent all values, I also know that within its pages are real stories of real lives. These stories may be a little porous, a little leaky and at times, they may challenge and disrupt. They may not always form the steadiest of vessels on which to float. But it is my hope that they will provide some buoyancy for readers treading water—readers who, like myself, occasionally need a raft to cling to.

Building blocks

Tom is about two years old and I am sitting with my friends, Lucy and Daniel, in the Botanic Gardens in Sydney. It is a humid summer day, hot and sticky like Sydney can be at this time of year. People are picnicking around us amid a cacophony of cockatoos screeching, children squealing, ferries on the harbour honking their horns. We're sprawled out on a rug with Tom, who is perched quietly like a little Buddha, contentedly watching the action around him, the leaves moving in the gum trees, the sun trickling through the branches. He is happy and relaxed and so am I. This is what I love about being a mother. Time to sit and appreciate the simple stuff. Before having a baby, I was a journalist and then a public relations consultant, rarely allowing myself time to stop, let alone sit on a rug in a sea of stillness and trees. I threw myself into yoga and meditation to stave off the inevitable stress that comes with full-time work, but it was all part of a carefully planned routine, not spontaneous, not a random moment like this. I do this a lot with Tom at this age: lie on a rug and read a book to him or stare up at the clouds. First child luxuries I suppose. From the day he was born, I was smitten and devoted. And I relished the time I took out from work to spend with my chubby, chilled-out baby. That easygoing nature has not changed in his toddler years.

Lucy jumps up and starts kicking a soft rubber ball to her son Liam, who is a few months older than Tom. Liam is running in pursuit of the ball and then starts to run away, laughing as Lucy calls to him and unsuccessfully pursues him in a game of chase. They duck between the bushes, dodging one another until Lucy finally catches Liam and tickles him into a state of giggly compliance.

Daniel looks to me and smiles. "He's very quiet, your Tom," he remarks. "We'd take Liam to the hospital if he just sat there like that."

What a funny thing to say, I think. Daniel's joking, but there's an honesty in the remark that stirs an uneasiness inside me, a moment of recognition. I suppose other children of the same age don't sit quietly content and observant for moments on end.

Don't they? Should I be worried? I don't remember anything else from that day, but the sense of worry lingered.

Soon after the picnic, I book tickets to a performance for toddlers at the Sydney Opera House. I go with my friend Amber and her two children and we decide to make a day of it, catching the train and having a picnic lunch in the sun. I am very pregnant with my second child and I relish the opportunity to have a special outing with Tom before the baby comes along.

The performance is a jazz ensemble, putting nursery rhymes to groovy music. As the music starts, Tom is sitting on my lap, pushing on my big belly, which is a little uncomfortable, but bearable. He doesn't want to sit with the other children down the front near the stage, but I totally empathise. I distinctly remember seeing a live performance of *The Wizard of Oz* at around the same age, and feeling quite intimidated. I had nightmares about it for days.

A performer in an incy-wincy spider costume appears in the wings. She creeps forward, waving her spindly arachnid arms around and then shouts SURPRISE! to the other performers who scream with glee. Apparently she surprises Tom too, who screams, and screams, and doesn't stop. He looks terrified and grabs at my body and my face until I stand up and carry him outside. I try distracting him with boats on the harbour, seagulls, food, anything to stop the screaming. He settles down, but every time I think he's ready to go back inside, he screams again, and even louder. Looking back, I think this was his first meltdown, and possibly the first time I felt completely flummoxed about how to respond. I was confused and mystified. We miss the rest of the performance and meet our friends afterwards.

It's odd. I remember feeling embarrassed about Tom's reaction and quite out of my depth. I can't help but compare Tom to all of the other children sitting quietly on the floor and I think 'why *my* child?' These days I am more accepting of Tom's quirks, but back then I was self-conscious and would often make comparisons. "I don't really know what just happened in there," I say to Amber later. We laugh, but detecting my fragility, she replies, "It's a sign of intelligence you know, when kids are sensitive like that." And I hold on to her words like a child clings to her mother's hand when she's in a crowd and is afraid of getting lost.

*

Baby Otis, like his big brother, arrives in a whirlwind. Two weeks early and fast enough for me to forget to ask for pain relief, my little Aquarius is born in a bathtub. Much to our surprise, he's a boy, even though we'd been told he was a girl in the ultrasound. It matters for a millisecond and then I cuddle and breastfeed my delectable baby boy, relishing his newborn aroma and gurgling sounds. Images of ballet classes, party dresses and mother-and-daughter time slip painlessly from my horizon, as I enjoy three blissful days in hospital getting to know my second bundle of boy and basking in a break from the routine of home.

After some six months of simultaneous nappies and potty training, breastfeeding and finger food, I make an appointment at the local community health clinic. Tom is three. The Botanic Gardens and Opera House incidents have been compounded by several other niggling concerns and I decide to run them by someone in the know. Perhaps Tom doesn't hear me when he should. Perhaps he doesn't look at people when he should. Perhaps he doesn't cope with daily challenges as he should. It's not really anything I can put my finger on, but a gut feeling tells me something is amiss. It's a feeling my husband James shares and it's compounded now that we have a second child on the scene. Are we doing something wrong from a parenting perspective? Or are we just being helicopter parents? Overly concerned? Overly protective? The internal questions are pervasive and cloud all my other thoughts.

The clinician is quick to dismiss my concerns. "He's reached all his developmental milestones," she enthuses. "He's holding eye contact with me. Look! See? Don't worry so much. All new parents worry."

I smile politely but secretly think, "He's holding eye contact with you because we're in a quiet room with no other distractions, you silly woman."

"Go home and make a nice cup of tea," she says in what I can't help but think is a patronising tone. And I go home feeling worse than I did before I came.

*

It's the 2007 federal election and Kevin Rudd is on the brink of being voted Australia's Prime Minister. We're having a weekend away, staying at a friend's cottage in a historic little coastal town called Catherine Hill Bay. The cottage is actually a rambling shack, filled to the brim with books and paintings, and it's a five-minute stroll to a great surf beach. James and our friend Josh have been surfing at sunrise and I've been taking long strolls along the sand alone, a sheer luxury after the intensity of caring for a toddler and baby.

James has gone to bed early and I'm watching the television and the carry-on that accompanies election night. Rather, I'm occasionally watching, but mostly, I'm engrossed in a *Sydney Morning Herald* magazine article. It's a feature article about a man who discovers he has Asperger's syndrome late in life. The words on the page reach out and touch me. They feel so familiar, as if I've read this article before, only I haven't. I say to Josh, who works as a health professional: "Have you heard of Asperger's?" In 2007, Asperger's, or 'high functioning' autism, as it later became known, wasn't often spoken about. Many people hadn't heard of it.

"Yep, I know about Asperger's," Josh replies.

"Do you reckon Tom might have it?" I casually ask, as if I'm asking if he wants his tea with milk or sugar.

"I've thought about that, you know," Josh says. "And maybe a year ago I would have suggested you follow it up. But I'm not sure now. His eye contact is better and he's more engaged. Maybe he just feels more comfortable around me. I don't know. Maybe it is worth getting a second opinion."

I'm shocked. He's actually considered this? Has he had this conversation with his wife, with other mutual friends? Do they know something I don't? I feel unsettled and nervous, as if I am teetering on the edge of a precipice. I turn back to the article, hungry for more information. Tom certainly ticks all the boxes: difficulty maintaining eye contact; an intense fascination with a special interest (he could write a PhD on Thomas the Tank Engine); meltdowns (off the Richter scale), sensory sensitivities and difficulty with fine and gross motor skills. But Tom is only three years old. How much of this is relatively normal for a toddler? Am I just being over-protective? Here comes that critical voice again. Was the community nurse right? Did I need to just chill out? But something shifts in me after reading this article and I decide that Josh is right. We need a professional opinion. I glance up at the television and hear Australia's outgoing leader John Howard conceding defeat after more than 11 years in power. Inside me, another tidal shift is taking a stronghold and gaining momentum.

On our return to Sydney, I book an appointment with a child psychologist at the aptly named clinic Quirky Kid. I am nervous, but confident this is the right thing to do. James and I instantly hit it off with the psychologist, who is our age, relaxed and friendly. Tom is happy because there are trains to play with. We share our concerns and feel supported in a way that we haven't before. She nods when we tell her how Tom becomes uncontrollably upset when he hears loud sounds, or how much he detests swimming classes. She smiles when we tell her how much he loves maps and how he can recite books word-for-word after just one reading. I tell her how terrible I feel when I can't find a way to calm him down. She chats to Tom and gets him to draw some pictures, all the while taking notes. She observes him flapping his hands when he gets excited, and how he becomes distracted by the moving leaves and tree branches outside her window. A couple of weeks later, she visits Tom at his childcare centre, speaking with his teachers and watching how he interacts with other children.

We return to the clinic and the psychologist confirms the diagnosis I had already privately made: Asperger's syndrome. She gives us a detailed report that assesses Tom using the Childhood Autism Rating Scale and suggests we confirm her findings with a paediatrician, which we later do. I don't remember feeling sad at the time. Perhaps I was. But overwhelmingly, I remember James and I collectively breathing a sigh of relief. All of those years of questioning our parenting, of grappling with confusing social scenarios, of dealing with intense meltdowns and not understanding why they were happening or what to do in response. Not only did we now have a reason, but we finally had support. It didn't come cheap, but for now, it felt like a warm security blanket had been wrapped around us both.

*

Around this time, Tom becomes fascinated in architecture, drawing cities and building them out of Duplo blocks. He doesn't like Lego because the pieces are too fiddly and he lacks the fine motor skills to manoeuver them. Walking into his bedroom becomes hazardous, for fear of knocking over precarious skyscrapers or treading on strategically placed cars or animals. He can spend hours on his own constructing these urban designs, stepping back for a bird's eye view every now and then, and adjusting his architectural sculptures one block at a time. One afternoon I pick him up from childcare, greeted at the door by a teacher, who says in a quiet voice: "Come and have a look at this." Tom has spent the afternoon constructing our local town hall with wooden blocks, complete with stage, dressing room, seats and upstairs viewing platform. I smile, nonplussed, having seen similar constructions many times before, but the educator appears amazed. "I hope you don't mind, but I have taken some photos to show our supervisor. I've never seen anything quite like this before. He's so creative." I feel overcome with pride and tell her to show the photos to whomever she likes.

*

Not long after our visit to the psychologist, I am in the grip of a research marathon. I jump on the internet and then quickly realise Dr Google is a shortcut to one big worry-fest. So I decide to invest in some reliable literature. The first book I buy is a handbook by the guru of Asperger's, Tony Attwood. It's a no-fuss textbook that tells it like it is. Children on the autism spectrum, he writes, might experience co-morbid conditions such as depression, anxiety, dyspraxia, ADHD, learning difficulties, Tourette's and epilepsy. I wrinkle my brow and read on. Even the word 'co-morbid' is somewhat morose. Looking back on Attwood's book now, I don't feel so nearly alarmed. But as a vulnerable mother of a newly-diagnosed Aspie, stories of prison, bullying and bouts of depression are not what I wanted to hear. Even still, each night I am a sponge as I soak up as much information as I can. I mark the pages I want James to read, but he's not interested. He'd rather "just accept Tom for who he is." I admire James's relaxed and non-judgmental attitude, but it also frustrates me no end, because how can we really know who Tom is if we don't understand how his little brain is wired? James didn't read any of the baby or parenting books I left, dog-eared, on his bedside table either. They simply gathered dust and coffee cup stains too.

I quickly accept that any research is going to fall into my domain. I also land the responsibility of pursuing therapy options, of which there are a ridiculous many. This job includes filtering out the charlatans and the ill-informed. Fluoride in the tap water, mercury, air pollution, parental stress when pregnant. It seems everything points to 'you stuffed up'. I am shocked at how many people feel inclined to offer a 'cause' or a 'cure'. One friend proffers the now-debunked theory that autism is caused by immunisation. In 1998 a paper in *The Lancet* connected autism with the measles-mumps-rubella (MMR) vaccine, prompting many parents to stop vaccinating their children. Other parents were blamed for already causing autism in their children by adhering to vaccination schedules.[8] It took 12 years for *The Lancet* to retract Andrew Wakefield's article on MMR vaccines, following years of investigation that pointed to fraud on his behalf. He also lost his medical license.[9] But by that stage the damage was well and truly done and the fallout continues today.

Our paediatrician warned me that people might raise this issue, equipping me with articles from scientific journals, just in case. I email my friend one of the articles after she raises the issue of vaccines with me, but she doesn't respond. I take that to mean she isn't interested in scientific evidence, only hearsay. I am shocked and angry. How does she think this makes me feel? I am struggling to come to terms with things and then she essentially accuses me of causing my son's autism because I tried to do the right thing and have him immunised. Since then, the matter has long been swept under the carpet and we remain friends. But a little part of me still feels disappointed whenever I remember.

Meanwhile, I continue to do my own questioning. Did I eat too much tinned tuna when I was pregnant? Do too much yoga in the third trimester? Too little? We struggled with breastfeeding in the first couple of days of his little life. Was that it? Attwood writes:

"parents should abandon feelings of personal guilt", that the brain of a person with high functioning autism is "wired differently, not necessarily defectively, and this was not caused by what a parent did or did not do during the child's development".[10] But for me, at least, it seems that guilt is all part of the process, the pathway to acceptance. I know I need to give myself a break, and give my son a break too. I'm just not sure how to go about doing that.

While most of our family members are incredibly supportive and understanding, other responses range from "he'll grow out of it" to "he just needs to be shown some boundaries." These comments are not helpful. They sit like a lead weight in the pit of my stomach. And at the same time, a number of people respond to Tom's diagnosis with statements like "Are you sure? He seems fine to me." To which James and I respond with "Yes, we are QUITE sure." This is where the "invisibility" of 'high functioning' autism sometimes comes into play, and the reason it has been dubbed "a hidden disability, because its symptoms are not always outwardly visible."[11]

As I write this, I am acutely aware that Tom will read it in the future, and may feel offended or, worse, demoralised. And rightly so. Is autism not just another way of being? Quite frankly, the way he sees the world is far more interesting than that of many people I know, myself included. He is a true artist in the way he observes his environment, the way he notices the detail in a building's façade, or the colours of a landscape. I know that parents of severely autistic children may disagree that autism is just another 'way of being' when they're still toilet training their eight year old or looking down the barrel of a lifetime as a carer. The spectrum is a broad one. But I can't help but think that for a child like Tom, so many of his difficulties revolve around how we as a society perceive difference. Difference makes us feel uncomfortable and challenges how we see ourselves.

Autism expert Simon Baron Cohen states: "Autism is both a disability and a difference. We need to find ways of alleviating the disability while respecting and valuing the difference".[12] Of course, the reality is that I want to equip Tom with the skills he needs to get by in society, and to grow up to be independent and happy. And this involves teaching him how to negotiate societal expectations and norms, as well as many other functional skills. Creativity and a curiosity are not enough to get by on in a world made for stereotypes of what constitutes 'normal'. This becomes even more apparent when Tom starts school and I quickly discover there is a blatant lack of resources in the public school system to cater for any child who falls outside of the norm. When he started school there was also a distinct lack of awareness, but I'm optimistic that this is changing.

I am reminded of a conversation I had with one of Tom's preschool teachers, who gave me some good advice (although I don't think I knew what to make of it at the time). She said: "Children like your boy are exceptional, but school is not easy for kids like him. Once he's finished school he can focus on his special interest and wow the world. Until then, you just gotta get him through the system." I can't count the number of times I've replayed that statement in my head.

Temples and towers

When Tom is in Year One, aged six, and Otis aged three, we decide to really test our stress levels and renovate our house. We've run out of room in our two-bedroom semi and need to expand. The walls of our 100-year-old home are crumbling, the plumbing is leaking and the kitchen cupboards have become unhinged. One night I stay up until 2 am painting over the yellow stains on the dining room wall, covering over years of grime with a slick of fresh, white paint and waking to the smell of fumes. But the remedy is short-lived. We are so over the place we've even stopped cleaning. It's time. We employ an architect and builder, both of whom are delightful and competent. I appoint myself Project Manager, which is a genuinely exciting prospect, while James and I pour over plans and revel in the creativity of choosing what our new renovated future might look.

This coincides with me leaving my part time job at a magazine, mostly because I feel I can't manage the day-to-day juggling act of work, picking up kids from childcare, and being everything to everyone. The clincher comes one day when, once again, I have to take a day off work to look after a sick child and my boss asks: "When's it going to be James's turn?" Unfortunately, if James takes a day off he doesn't get paid. While his freelancing work sounds flexible, the reality is quite different. Working in the TV industry also means James is working long hours and travelling for weeks at a time. Family friendly it is not. But with a hefty Sydney mortgage, a renovation in the pipeline and ongoing therapy costs, we need the money.

We move to a rental house for the six-month period of the renovation. This house is affectionately known as the 'pit of despair' or the 'house of gloom'. It's cheap and nasty, and stuck on the edge of a suburb that feels like nowhere. With few friends nearby and our family mostly on the other side of the country, we might as well be living in a desert. There is a big backyard, which is an advantage with two active little boys. But one of the cons is that it's a very hot summer and the house is not insulated, let alone air-conditioned. In short, it feels like a pressure cooker, literally and metaphorically, all of the time. One weekend the thermometer reaches 45 degrees Celsius. Inside the house it's like a sauna and the four of us are red-faced and very grumpy. I spend much of that summer sitting in the outdoor paddle pool with a glass of wine in my hand.

On the upside, Otis and Tom have developed a very endearing sibling relationship. It is a delight to listen in on their conversations about Star Wars or dinosaurs or witness them act out imaginary scenes on the trampoline. Otis is a super energetic preschooler, challenging the boundaries at every opportunity. Tom, meanwhile, is having a tough time socially. At school he's become quite introverted and spends lunchtimes by himself, eating on his own and then pacing in the playground. His teachers think of him as quiet and withdrawn, yet on his return home from school every day he chews my ear off with facts and figures about geography, natural disasters or world affairs, with all of the intensity and wisdom of a little professor. When I'm too busy to listen, he tells it to his little brother, who listens, or at least pretends to. We could give Tom all the therapy in the world and he still wouldn't develop the social skills, or receive the unconditional love he gets from Otis, reciprocated in double doses. Later, this affection comes in the form of a dog, an oversized Welsh Springer Spaniel, another form of therapy that money can't buy.

Unfortunately, Tom's professorial conversational skills do not translate to children's parties and I have to stay on full alert at social gatherings in case he has a meltdown. We inevitably leave such parties early. Sometimes it is a struggle to simply get in the door. I now realise that at these times Tom was experiencing crippling social anxiety and panic attacks. On one occasion we travelled across the city to a children's birthday party by the harbour. James is away, or working as he often is on these occasions. As we arrive we are greeted by the din of happy voices and edge tentatively down the driveway toward the gathering. There is a paperbark tree adorned with Chinese lanterns. Adults are sipping champagne from plastic cups. But as we draw closer Tom digs in his heels, pulling at my skirt. "I want to go home," he says in a shaky voice. Otis runs ahead to join a group of children playing backyard cricket with makeshift wickets made of driftwood, their laughs and squeals suddenly amplified.

"I can't do it," Tom whispers, tears starting to flood his eyes. "I'm telling the truth." I mentally unpack the psychologist's toolkit of strategies, but struggle to remember what she said. "Let's take some deep breaths together," I hopelessly offer. "We can do this." The hosts have spotted us and I can feel their eyes on me. I suggest Tom sit calmly and wait until he's ready to join us. "Breathe. Count to three. Think positive thoughts," I throw his way in a last ditch effort. But he's not ready and scrambles into some bushes and waits, the look on his face a mix of terror and sadness. I leave him there and feel awful. My first mouthful of champagne tastes bitter, but I swallow it greedily. I eventually manage to coax him out of his hiding place, but neither of us is in the party mood that day and we leave not long after.

Transitions, new places and new faces are always particularly tricky. Prior to going anywhere I try to prep Tom for any surprises—who will be there and what might transpire. I'm also constantly on watch to encourage him to join in to, or prompt, conversation with other children. Needless to say, I am always on alert and never really relax.

On one occasion, when Tom is about seven we decide a trip up to the Blue Mountains outside of Sydney could be fun. I pack a lunch and together with the two boys we start the ascent via train from Central. As we approach the mountains, passing blue gums and heritage cottages, Tom cries: "It's raining and misty! We won't be able to see the mountains!" There are raindrops splattering the window and mist is rolling over the valley, creating, what I think, is a magical sense of mystique and romance. But Tom has a picture in his head of what the mountains would look like and this is not it. "I don't want to go any-more. I want to get off, off, off!" he screams to the passengers on the train carriage. I am embarrassed, indignant and disappointed. Whereas once his behavior could have been passed off as a toddler tantrum, he is now too old for such carry on, I think. I'm worried Tom will ruin our special day out—this is not what I had in mind either. Otis too is starting to get upset, so I cuddle him closer and hold back my tears. "Why do you always have to be so negative?" I hear myself say to Tom. "Just enjoy it for what it is." I want to say more but bite my tongue, aware of the other passengers. After what seems like a very long journey, we arrive in Katoomba and right on cue the sun comes out. The Three Sisters greet us with their majesty and the kookaburras sing our welcome. We relish a day of bushwalking and breathtaking scenery after all, but I am rattled by Tom's outburst, and even more so by mine.

Tom and I can now both laugh about this story, seeing the ridiculousness of the situation. We also now both recognise that things don't always go to plan. He tells me that he tries not to look forward to things, because he might just end up being disappointed. While this makes me feel a little sad, I also admire the awareness he has around his emotions and the clever survival tactics he's developed. And in many ways, I've adopted the same strategy.

I find this time in our lives really difficult to write about. It was messy and confusing. I felt beset with loneliness, despite the fact I had two small children with me all of the time. Reality was hard to take but Bombay Sapphire Gin helped, or so I thought. I was drinking daily, by myself. As the months went on, gin o'clock crept forward and my pours were getting bigger. James was also self-medicating, his propensity for fine red wine becoming insatiable. At a bottle or two a night, he was inevitably either drunk or hungover, and it was starting to eat away at our relationship, not to mention our budget. I started feeling resentful of him because his work allowed him time away—resentful of the whole situation I had found myself in. I felt trapped.

I realise how dire this all sounds. But somehow, in the midst of it all, our family was still a loving little unit with laughs, music, dancing, books and friends. I found video footage of Tom's seventh birthday recently, while looking for something on my computer. In the video, Tom has a wide smile, proud as punch to be surrounded by friends who are holding balloons and singing him happy birthday. The children gather around a cake I have made in the shape of a giant seven, a recipe from the *Women's Weekly*. Little Otis is by Tom's side and I can hear James's laughs behind the video camera. Reveling in the attention, Tom blows out the candles and when I suggest he makes a wish, he replies: "I wish...I wish that it was my birthday every day!" to which the crowd erupts in laughter. It is such a beautiful moment and, dare I say, all very 'normal'. It makes me wonder if my memory of the hard times is over-inflated, for Tom seems like a perfectly happy little kid. Maybe things weren't as tough as I remember. Maybe I am just dwelling on the negatives. But then again, I guess every day was not his birthday, not at all.

The renovations were finished on time and on budget, and we survived the 'pit of despair', marriage intact. I would even go so far as to say the experience fortified our relationship as a couple, and as a family. It most certainly opened up the channels of communication. I'd like to think we became better at talking about our emotions. We took to having family meetings around the dinner table, taking turns to raise issues that were bugging us and trying to collectively iron them out, our kids included in the decision-making. While some conversations were confronting and awkward, other times we talked with familiarity and ease. I seem to remember James and I had many arguments brought on by my resentment about having to carry so much of the parenting and housework load. I know he took his role as breadwinner very seriously and often came home from work drained of all energy. Often we would battle head-to-head for the title of 'most exhausted'. Some discussions ended in tears; but others ended in hugs.

As I write this I get a knot in my stomach that won't go away. I worry that people will judge my family and my son, whom I want to protect. And I worry that putting this stuff out there is the wrong thing to do. But if I don't, and if I don't talk about the chaos and confusion, who else is going to? It makes me feel uncomfortable but I'm not going to gloss over it and pretend it's all a bed of roses. When things are going swimmingly, it seems like none of this really matters. But when we're going through a hard patch, if Tom is going through a bout of anxiety, if I feel like I'm spinning out of control, or I read about yet another teenager who has committed suicide because of bullying, I feel a renewed need to share our story. Maybe another family is going through tough times and will read this and realise they are not alone. It can be intense but eventually the tempests pass. I'm not saying that having a child on the spectrum was the reason for all the difficulties in our life at this time. There were very many contributing factors. But I do think the dynamic of caring for a child with a disability adds to a family's stress levels. It has certainly contributed to my sense of feeling stuck and isolated, my feeling that there wasn't really anyone who understood.

*

Around the time Tom turns eight he becomes very interested in temples, particularly Angkor Wat in Cambodia. He is interested in Buddhism and reads out facts and figures on Angor Wat's religious origins, its size and architectural features. He explores it on Google Earth too and, of course, draws it with crayons, pencils, whatever we have lying around. Friends have recently moved to Phnom Penh and, knowing about Tom's interest in temples, send us a postcard of Angkor Wat, which I paste onto the front cover of his homework book. It is a classic photograph of the temple complex at sunrise, a clear reflection over the lake, the morning sky and water emanating shades of orange, purple and pink. Tom ogles the postcard at any opportunity. You could say it has become an obsession.

We decide to embrace Tom's deep interest and take a family holiday to Cambodia. In fact, most of our holidays have been shaped around Tom's enthusiasm for a particular culture or destination at the time. Not only does it guarantee that he will be engaged on holidays, but it means he can also help plan an itinerary and prepare himself for what's to come. In Cambodia we firstly stay with our friends in Phnom Penh, enjoying their local knowledge and exploring the south of the country. We stay at a resort called Les Manguiers (The Mangoes), which looks across a river edged by gold-spired temples and rice fields to misty tropical mountains. We then fly to Siem Reap, where, with the help of a tour guide, visit temple upon temple. Tom revels in every moment, taking thousands of photographs along the way. His enthusiasm is charming, but exhausting. Otis is very patient, but on one occasion, exhausted by the prospect of yet another temple, he and I opt to stay by the hotel pool and have pedicures and mocktails while James and Tom do more exploring.

We save Angkor Wat as our final destination. It is to be our pièce de résistance. It is also Otis's sixth birthday and we consider it a fitting way to celebrate. We plan to watch the sunrise, have a tour of the grounds and then go on an elephant ride, which is Otis's birthday present. Our guide picks us up from the hotel at 4.30am and after driving to the site we shuffle in the darkness to the edge of the lake, sensing other tourists around us, all waiting in suspense for the first glimmer of light. Whispers in a multitude of languages subside as the sun creeps above the horizon. Click, click, click go the cameras as the sun rises higher. It is only in the light of sunrise that I realise how many other people are here. We are surrounded by masses of tourists from every part of the globe. "Happy birthday," I whisper to Otis and peck a kiss on his cheek. Then a cry rings out: "It's cloudy! It's cloudy!" James and I look at each other, and then to Tom. "Shhhhhhh" we say in unison. He is crying, loudly, writhing and stomping his feet, for the Angkor Wat image before our eyes is not the one on the front of his homework book. "It's cloudy! This is not what it's meant to look like!" his distressed voice pierces the silence. The moment of serenity has dissipated and in its place is a full-blown meltdown. I feel my anger and stress levels rising. "Why now? In this beautiful place, this once-in-a-lifetime opportunity?" Even the other tourists are shooshing us and fair enough, for I am all too aware of how much money these people have paid to be here. After quickly taking some obligatory photos, we escape the throng and walk toward some monks in orange robes, smiling at us quizzically. It takes a good hour for Tom to settle down, but he eventually does, awestruck, as we all are, by Angkor Wat's temples and all that has gone before them. Later, we have a picnic by the waters of the giant moat that surrounds the temples—looking across to the ancient city from a distance, in a new light.

Returning back to that time, I can see that the build-up was ridiculous. The pressure to have a good time was too great, and the picture-perfect postcard image, not to be. It did, however, teach us a lesson about expectations. While it is good to look forward to something, it is also important to accept what comes your way. Just as Tom needed to let go of his image of Angkor Wat, I have needed to let go of the child I thought I was going to have. Instead I have embraced the child before me and, in fact, he has surpassed my expectations. We wouldn't have been in Cambodia if it weren't for him. We wouldn't have visited Angkor Wat if it weren't for his passion for all things Cambodian and Buddhist, all things architectural and worldly. Tom recognises the beauty in life that many of us neglect to see. He brings a sense of curiosity, excitement and purpose to adventures that would otherwise not exist. And for that I am exceedingly grateful.

*

My favourite photo of Tom is taken in Brooklyn on our first day in New York. Aged 10, he is standing, jaw agape, eyes wide, seeing Manhattan's iconic cityscape for the first time. Christmas in New York had been a long-held dream of mine, but the holiday was largely instigated by Tom, who'd been infatuated with the city since about the age of three. Ever the artist, he had drawn the skyline for years, read up on the city's history, studied the skyscrapers, the beautiful art deco detail of the Chrysler and the Empire State Buildings, and scoured all the streets of New York on Google Earth. "How could we not take him there?" James and I both surmised, and somehow saved up the airfare and organised the logistics.

Tom's enthusiasm for architecture is never more apparent than on that first day. Still groggy from a lead-weight afternoon sleep, we take to the streets. With all the curiosity of fresh tourists, we wander randomly past Peter Pan Donuts, Steve's Meats and sidewalk Christmas tree stalls. We are housesitting a friend's place in Williamsburg and the buildings are shrouded in an orange hue as the day runs out of light. The air is crisp, but the promised winter frost has not yet set in. We see the tips of skyscrapers in the distance and find ourselves lured toward the water, down a street of brownstones adorned with pine cone wreaths and fairy lights and past a beer factory smelling of hops.

Leading the charge is Tom, his enthusiasm and sense of urgency heightened as the sunlight quickly dissipates. Keeping pace is little Otis, and then James, all of us keen to discover what is around the next corner. Our strides quicken, the anticipation almost too much. A quick turn left, another right and then we find ourselves running across a grassy park toward a pier, the perfect vantage point for seeing the Manhattan cityscape we all know so well from the sketches on paper always at the kitchen table. What had felt like an unrealistic obsession for a young boy on the other side of the world now feels very real and right. "It's even more beautiful than I imagined it would be," Tom enthuses, the grin on his face saying it all. We all laugh, relieved, knowing it could have gone either way. A friendly bearded man takes our family portrait, sensing the enormity of the moment and capturing the cinematic auburn lighting. We are guided by the tenacity of one little artist with a New York obsession, but the vision has become ours as a family, and this feeling of togetherness is tangible. On the way back home we stop for tacos and doughnuts and stay up late chatting like four excitable kids at a sleepover.

*

By the end of primary school, Tom was ready to move on. He applied for a high school that specialises in visual art, diligently worked on his portfolio, nailed his interview and was ecstatic when he was accepted. But it wasn't to be. I hesitate to say more, but essentially there was bullying involved. Tom's mood plummeted and I can safely say it was the most stressed I have ever been. Each morning I woke after another terrible night's sleep, with a sense of dread about sending Tom through those school gates. James was also terribly upset and so we decided to pull the pin and unenrol him before the term finished. People have said that withdrawing him from the school must have been a difficult decision to make, but the decision was the easy part.

Thankfully Tom was accepted into a good local high school where he had friends from primary school. These are boys who understand Tom's quirks and his need for space and genuinely appreciate him as a confidante. Tom has been at this school since and he gets more support than he did at the previous high school. But it hasn't been easy.

I have to constantly remind myself that marks don't matter—that he has his own learning style, he needs to take things at his own pace, and that mainstream schools are, in reality, made for 'mainstream' kids. I've come to accept that Tom is constantly going to have a full 'in tray' and that not all homework will be done or assignments handed in. That's not an easy thing for me to accept, as a diligent student myself. Some days I am positively beside myself when he rejects my requests for him to do his homework or I open his books and see pages of drawings instead of notes. Homework has ended in tears too many times to count (his and mine). Some days are too hard and we give up, because no homework is worth that much angst. Other days, if he succeeds in getting an assessment done, he might forget to hand it in, because the "teacher didn't ask" or rather, he missed the instruction. This then involves me chasing his teachers to ask for an extension. It is all very time consuming and frustrating.

Tom needs time to emotionally regulate, to unwind at the end of a tiring day in a school with one thousand noisy children. And this is compounded by a busy schedule of tutoring and therapy. I know all of this, and yet I still find myself getting hooked into an academic environment that sees many students stressed out of their minds all for the sake of a ticket to university. I constantly catch myself projecting into the future, worrying what that might look like if he doesn't finish this here assignment on the archeology of Petra or master trigonometry in time for next week's exam. I'm also not afraid to admit that it's as much about me feeling like a failure as it is about him. My perfectionism takes a right battering.

Of course, I know what matters most is Tom's happiness. And in the good moments I do have faith that he will find his way in life. That it will be okay. I also remind myself, again and again, of his preschool teacher's comments that I've just "gotta get him through the system".

Being a university tutor myself, I know how difficult—though not impossible—Tom would be to teach. While Tom loves to learn, it is generally only about things he's interested in, topics that hold his attention. Many of the subjects simply don't float his boat and getting him to work on those is near impossible. The key is to tap into his interests. One afternoon he came bursting through the door after school, reached into his bag and presented me with a map of the world he'd been working on in geography. He had filled in all of the names of the countries in the tiniest of handwriting—all of them, that is, "except the countries that were too small to write in". He knew them all off by heart after so many years of examining maps and atlases and Google Earth. 'Hyperfocus' is what the experts call this ability to spend so long focusing on detail while excluding other distractions. "Incredible! That's wonderful," I enthused, for it really was an extraordinary feat and one I could never accomplish. "Is that what you were actually meant to do?" I sheepishly asked. "I'm not sure," was the reply. He really had no idea what the task was. But I didn't care. He was glowing and happy and proud.

It does seem to me that schools could take more of a strength-based approach to kids like Tom, rather than dwelling on deficits or challenges. Aside from helping them to stay on task, a strengths-based approach boosts self-esteem and confidence. What is the point of writing on a report card for a kid with ADHD that he "needs to pay more attention"? We all know that! In his seminal book *The Explosive Child*, clinical child psychologist Ross W. Greene writes that we can't expect the atypical child to change. Instead, we need to change ourselves. "Children do well if they can," he writes. "If they can't, we need to figure out why, so we can help."[13] This correlates to the idea of the 'social model of disability', which suggests that it is not the disabled person who needs to change their way of being, but rather, society needs to change to accommodate diversity. As the late Stella Young, disability advocate and comedian, described it; "we are more disabled by the society we live in than by our bodies and our diagnoses." She went on to tell a TEDx audience in 2014:

> No amount of smiling at a flight of stairs has ever made it turn it into a ramp. Smiling at a television screen isn't going to make closed captions appear for people who are deaf. No amount of standing in the middle of a book-shelf and radiating a positive attitude is going to turn all those books into braille. It's just not going to happen. I really want to live in a world where disability is not the exception, but the norm.[14]

I was thrilled last year when one teacher wrote a positive comment on Tom's report card, recognising his 'creativity and adaptability'. Ironically, however, it is the teacher who should be applauded for his 'adaptability'. He recognised Tom's strengths and allowed him to use a different computer program to his peers—one that he was competent and confident with, resulting in an excellent project. Such initiative, on the part of a teacher, keeps me buoyed. Ideally, though, adaptability shouldn't be the "exception, but the norm". It is a teacher's job, albeit a challenging and frustrating one at times, to find the learning style that best suits a student.

What Tom really needs at school is someone to keep him on track and organised; to ensure that when he's feeling anxious he can take time out; to prompt him if there is a group activity and he is reluctant to join in. It's a big job and the hardworking support teacher in his class does it wonderfully, assisting several children with learning needs. Support is everything. And yet, it seems there is never enough to go around. Teachers in public schools are spread thin. Also, I often wonder how many children are slipping through the gaps—children who may not have support at home, whose parents are not confident when it comes to liaising with the school, or who may not be able to afford tutoring or therapy costs.

While I do, on the most part, feel supported by our school, there have been some misunderstandings and challenging times. And on more than one occasion, I have been known to stay up late at night Googling alternatives, from independent schools to homeschooling (budget constraints and logistics aside). Tom, however, wants to stay put. To his credit, he tells me he wants to be "educated in a mainstream school with everyone else" and stay at the school where his friends are—he has some lovely friends too. So I am on a mission to make it work, because like him, I believe he has the right to a decent education at a public school, where his people are. His community.

We are all social beings seeking bonds with like-minded individuals, striving to find a tribe—even if that is a more challenging prospect for some. By happenstance, I have managed to find my tribe in the process of writing this book. Through interviewing the families in the chapters that follow, I have found characters who, like me, have waded through the ambiguity and quagmire, and who are possibly richer for it. After all, it is through this collective sharing of stories that we have come to understand and appreciate the everyday.

Same but different

Jacinta & Zac

In the lounge room of this suburban Brisbane home are three large blue armchairs. One belongs to Jacinta, another to her husband Steve and the third, their 12 year old son Zac. The house is comfortable and welcoming, free from flashy trimmings. A balmy afternoon breeze drifts through an open window, rustling some papers at the end of the table where Jacinta has been working from home. Alongside her paperwork is a bolt of brightly-coloured upholstery fabric and a sewing machine, which Jacinta likes to use when she's not working. Zac will often sit alongside her, playing computer games as she sews or embroiders.

"Computers, computers, computers," laughs Jacinta when I ask her about Zac's interests. "He'll probably end up working in computers. But we have a little way to go before then. He also loves movies and he'll tell you intricate details about what plotline or what sequence of dialogue went on in a movie—particularly action movies, and myths and legends. He doesn't like romance, kissing and that type of thing is a bit yucky. But that's pretty age appropriate, I think."

As we are chatting, a builder comes to the door to discuss the family's plans to renovate. Jacinta explains that she wants to make some more space and privacy for Zac as he becomes an adolescent. She is conscious that he needs some quiet downtime in amongst his busy schedule of homework, swimming and fencing classes. He also does a personal training session with Jacinta and Steve once a week, helping to improve his coordination and keep his weight down. "He can't get out of it if we all do it together," Jacinta laughs. "And I think he enjoys doing stuff together as a family."

She goes on to tell me that Zac is an empathic and affectionate child, dispelling the stereotype of children on the spectrum not wanting to be touched. Diagnosed with an ASD at age seven, he rebuts many of the stereotypes about autism, including the theory that people on the spectrum are loners.

"Zac's an extrovert and loves making friends, and being around people," explains Jacinta. "He is a very kind child with a lot to give, but sometimes he loses the plot and so his friendships are always very turbulent. He wants to be friends with people but doesn't understand why they don't want to be friends with him, which can be quite disturbing for him."

At this moment, Zac, who has been in his bedroom playing on his phone, enters the room and sits at the table with us. He looks to Jacinta as if waiting for instructions as she introduces us. "Hello, how are you? Very nice to meet you," he says in a somewhat formal voice, with a slight British accent. He then rather abruptly stands, saying: "I'll be heading off now to see my friend Harry. He lives two doors up the road. Mum arranged a get-together so you two could talk about me in private."

Jacinta and I both laugh. "No point beating around the bush. Best to tell it like it is," she says. "Right-o then. Bye!" Zac leans over and gives his Mum a warm embrace before heading out the door. "He's a very cuddly and loving boy, always has been," continues Jacinta when she thinks Zac is out of earshot.

"He has Sensory Integration Disorder as part of his autism, so all of his senses are heightened. Sometimes that gets to him and he becomes overwhelmed. His sense of smell is unbelievable. So is his eyesight, and that goes for touch as well. Unlike some autistic children who don't like to be touched, he actually seeks these things out. He's a seeker, a sensate."

It is clear they have a close bond, Jacinta and Zac, and that she knows her son well. "Perhaps a little too well," she jokes. But it has been a journey getting to know him over the years. Throughout his primary school years, Zac has always been known as 'that' kid. If there is a ruckus in the classroom, everyone looks at Zac, even if he hasn't caused it. If someone is hurt in the playground, the teachers look to see where Zac is. When he was a preschooler, he would hit or push other children out of frustration and quickly secured a reputation as 'the naughty kid'. It is a reputation he still can't seem to shake, despite a vast improvement in his behavior, the culmination of therapy and medication for anxiety and ADHD. Now in Year Six, he's looking forward to starting afresh at a new high school next year, an exclusive private school, where no one knows his history. Jacinta is also looking forward to a fresh start next year. She is weary and hopes that Zac will be better understood by the adults and children at his new school.

"We keep saying to him, 'clean slate mate'," says Jacinta. "We tell him it's his opportunity to not have any history come with him. 'You are who you are. You're not the three-year-old everybody remembers. You're not the five-year-old that everybody remembers. You're Zac and you are who you are.'"

In the meantime, however, he still has primary school demons to face. With a shock of red hair and a rotund frame he is like a beacon in the playground. And because he is easily provoked, the other children often taunt him to get a reaction. They find it funny to watch him go pink in the face and work up beads of sweat on his upper lip. They snigger when he jumps up and down, and when he is told off by the teachers and sent to the principal's office. Often, by the time he gets there, he is so overwhelmed he can't even speak. On some days, he gets detention and has to sit in the school foyer until the end of lunch, trying not to cry or stand up and walk around. The foyer is old-fashioned and cold. There is no soft furnishing so sounds echo off the walls. Zac watches the passing parade of children and teachers, who eyeball him because they know he's in trouble again. He probably knows this foyer better than any other kid in the school and he can't wait to kiss it goodbye at the end of the year.

Jacinta and Steve took Zac to see his first psychologist at age three. They were working full time and Zac was attending family day care. The carer was a gentle, capable woman, but she one day rang Jacinta and told her that she could no longer look after Zac. Instead, she suggested, he should attend a preschool where there were several carers to manage his behavior.

"She told us that he was lashing out at other kids, that he would incite riots," says Jacinta. "He was a runner too and he would take off and then the other kids would take off, so she had five little kids all taking off in different directions. At home he would hit us and he was strong. It would hurt. God knows what he was doing to children when he was getting frustrated, because he hurt me, so he must have really been hurting other kids."

It would be easy to write Zac's behavior off as defiance, but Jacinta knew there was more to it. She read parenting manuals from cover to cover and tried sticker charts and other reward systems. She tried consequences, taking away his favourite toy or restricting screen time, but that could set Zac off on a tantrum that could last a full hour. Advice from the typical parenting manuals didn't seem to work with Zac. Jacinta started avoiding noisy places and other situations that might set him off. "He's super sensitive to sound," she says. "You can't whisper in the house because 'old bat ears' will pick it up. 'Why did you say that? Why are you whispering?' he says. You have to be careful what you say."

Jacinta found herself declining invitations to social events because she knew they would be too much. Inevitably they left birthday parties early, just before Zac had a meltdown—or sometimes, soon after. She and Steve tried adhering to strict routines, drawing timetables up and sticking them on the fridge. Meal-times and activities were at the same set time every day. It did seem that the more structure Zac had in his life, the better behaved he was, to some extent anyway. But every strategy eventually unfurled in some way or another. Jacinta spoke to the preschool teachers who agreed Zac was a challenging child.

"They said there is a social issue," explains Jacinta. "They couldn't tell us what it was, but they knew there was an issue and suggested we see a psychologist for advice."

Jacinta and Steve took the day off work, picked Zac up from preschool and set off. The psychologist, recommended by a friend, was based across town, a good two hour round trip. Once there, they ran through a series of questionnaires, chatted, cried and waited. Eventually, the psychologist told them that Zac had met the markers for a diagnosis of Oppositional Defiant Disorder (ODD).

"Well, that was confronting," says Jacinta. "When I read up on ODD, it was basically just bad parenting. I thought, you know, I don't have tickets on myself but I don't think so. We're trying very hard here, very hard. They said you've got to be consistent. I said how much more consistent? We live in a very regimented house because we have to. Yes, he's an only child, but does that make me a helicopter parent worrying over nothing? Yes, I work full time, but does that make me a negligent parent? There's so much judgment wrapped up in a diagnosis like that."

Meanwhile Jacinta also felt judged by those closest to her—her parents, and members of Steve's family, many of whom were from a medical background. They didn't overtly criticise her, but small comments about her parenting style did not go unnoticed.

"I was getting the feeling that they were thinking 'you only have one child and you're trying to make something up that he doesn't have'. But I don't think they realised how much we were really coping with. I knew that other families weren't experiencing the same things. Other families didn't have a child who was too terrified to walk down the hallway to the toilet. Other families weren't getting phone calls from teachers or having to deal with hour-long meltdowns. We're both fairly educated people and fairly well versed in how things work, and we knew that things were harder than they were supposed to be. We knew he didn't fit into a pigeonhole. He wasn't withdrawn, he could read, and walk and run from a very early age. He was capable in many ways but we knew there were gaps.

"He had a partial meltdown with my mum one day and that's when I think she got it. It's not that she hadn't believed me before then, but she would say things like 'why won't he eat green vegetables? You and your brother ate green vegetables'. But after having him for a few sleepovers she realised that you could do anything you like with this kid and he wasn't going to eat green vegetables. Lots of kids don't eat vegetables, I know that, but with Zac, it was something else! And my Mum witnessed that. Feeding him was a nightmare. Give him a stew and you'd think someone was trying to kill him. The smell, the taste, the texture, he just wouldn't cope with the sensory overload. He likes baked chicken now. He likes chips. He likes grilled fish, nothing on it. Plain, plain, plain food."

Feeling the need for a second opinion, Jacinta took Zac to see another psychologist. By this stage he was aged about five. Zac struck up a rapport with this psychologist and continued to see her regularly for the next few years. Jacinta was pleased to be getting support, but reports were still coming back from preschool, and then primary school. He was also seeing an occupational therapist, on the recommendation of his kindergarten teacher. "His teacher, who was gorgeous, said 'we have to do something about his handwriting. It is totally illegible. It was because Zac had very low muscle tone and very slack ligaments so holding a pencil was incredibly difficult and he got very tired. The OT was terrific, really very good, and his handwriting is lovely now. He's slow with writing, but it's very neat. So we got that sorted out, but other things would come up, physical issues, so we'd sort it out, like working through a checklist. But still the social stuff was happening."

Around the time Zac turned seven, the family took a holiday to Malaysia. They saw orangutans in the jungles of Borneo and visited friends in Kuala Lumpur. The Muslim community was celebrating the end of Ramadan with the Eid Festival and there were many Middle Eastern tourists on holiday. On one occasion, the family visited a shopping centre with Jacinta's friend. It was busy and noisy and many of the women were clothed in full burqa with just their eyes showing.

"That freaked him out," remembers Jacinta. "Although some autistic children can't read body language or facial expressions very well, what do they do if there's nothing to read? If there are just eyes and just black hills of fabric? Not to mention he was out of his own environment, in a foreign country.

"We were at an indoor play centre in the middle of the shopping centre when he proceeded to have the most almighty meltdown. There was Steve and I, and my lovely friend, and it was blood, sweat, tears and snot. Zac was on the floor flailing about and I just thought, how do we get out of here? Thankfully my friend was from a wealthy background and they had a family driver. She got the driver to go downstairs to the bottom of the lift and somehow, I don't know how because he was all floppy, a screaming boneless mess, we managed to get him into the lift and back to the hotel into his big bed in front of the TV. It took him about three hours to calm down. And the rest of the holiday was spent making mercy dashes back to the hotel to watch Cartoon Network."

Jacinta now realises that Zac was experiencing emotional and sensory overload, but at the time she didn't understand the complexity of the situation. Ross W. Greene breaks down the specifics of a meltdown in his book *The Explosive Child*, identifying that a meltdown experienced by an "inflexible-explosive" child, as he puts it, is quite distinct from a tantrum experienced by a neurotypical child:

> Obviously, *meltdown* is not an original term; go to any playground frequented by two-year-olds and you'll hear their parents describing, often with good humor, their children's latest 'meltdown of the week'. The meltdowns of inflexible-explosive children often look very much like those of two-year-olds. But the parents of inflexible-explosive children do not describe meltdowns with good humor. They've been enduring them for a long time, and the meltdowns have become much more frequent, intense, and uncontrollable.[15]

The meltdown, Greene writes, is a by-product of an inability to be flexible or tolerate frustration, when a child is beyond the toddler-years. He writes that the phenomenon has also been termed "neural hijacking" or "disintegrative rage", due to the incoherence and sheer lack of rationality exhibited during a meltdown, usually resulting in destructive, abusive behavior. It is not pleasant for the person having a meltdown, nor for the people witnessing it. Greene insists that there is no point in trying to discipline or teach a child during a meltdown as they simply will not be in a state to learn. Reasoning, insisting, punishing or berating on the part of a parent are all pointless. Letting the child have space, quiet and time for emotional regulation is key, but sometimes this is difficult to achieve.

Such was the case with Zac's episode in Malaysia. It rattled Jacinta so much she decided to seek a third opinion upon the family's return to Australia. She took Zac to see a psychiatrist (recommended by his psychologist), and it was then that things started to make sense. Zac was diagnosed with PDD-NOS [Pervasive Developmental Disorder-Not Otherwise Specified]. "The psychiatrist just said, yep, he's on the spectrum," recalls Jacinta. By this stage he was seven and a half, and it was four years after she first sought professional help—four years of worry and confusion.

Like Asperger's, PDD-NOS used to be a separate diagnosis to autism, until changes to the Diagnostic and Statistical Manual of Mental Disorders (DSM V) in 2013 saw them folded into the diagnosis of autism spectrum disorder. PDD-NOS was sometimes used when children did not meet all of the criteria for an autism spectrum disorder, or displayed mild symptoms. Of course, these things are never black and white, and PDD-NOS can occur in conjunction with other conditions, such as ADHD or Sensory Processing Disorder. But for Jacinta and Steve the diagnosis was a good start. They both agreed that it explained Zac's social difficulties, his low muscle tone and slack ligaments, his sensory issues and his meltdowns. One piece of advice that the psychiatrist gave them was to never go "head-to-head" with Zac, or this would incite an almighty explosion. Contrary to the advice of a previous therapist, who suggested forcing Zac to try new and different foods every day, this psychologist said that Zac should be allowed to try them when he was ready. This echoes Ross Greene's formula "inflexibility + inflexibility = meltdown". He writes, "[h]elping your child be more flexible usually means that you will have to be more flexible first."[16]

Up until this point of the interview, Jacinta has struck me as pragmatic. Stoic even. So when she bursts into tears I am surprised. I am taken aback by her show of raw emotion as she reaches for the tissues and speaks in choked sentences. She explains that while she felt relieved to get the final diagnosis, she also felt terribly sad, still feels sad. I understand. Oh boy, do I understand. But at the same time, her response stops me in my tracks because it makes me realise how long it's been since I felt sad about Tom's diagnosis. Perhaps I am at a different stage of the grieving process. Perhaps I have arrived at acceptance, although I would be lying if I said there weren't still days when I wanted to cry. I think researching and writing this book has helped with that process. It has helped me to somewhat rationalise things, to feel less overwhelmed by the impending doom and gloom that a diagnosis can imply, and it has helped me realise kids on the spectrum can have terrific futures and fulfilling childhoods as well.

Jacinta knows this too of course, as she goes through the daily motions of caring for her child. But as I speak to her, I can sense that recounting the time of the diagnosis is tough. Steve's mother had died three weeks prior to Zac's diagnosis so the family was already emotionally vulnerable. "On the outside I was holding it together, but I would let my guard down with the people closest to me," Jacinta recalls. "My brother was really lovely. He said 'he's still the same kid he was yesterday, it's just that he's got a label. And you love him just the same.' I said 'yep I sure do'. He said 'he's the same but different'."

I tell Jacinta that I used to constantly worry about the future. Would Tom be able to have a career? Would he be able to find a partner? Such thoughts would keep me awake at night. Of course it's completely irrational to worry about something that hasn't happened yet, something we know nothing about, but to some degree, as a parent you can't help it. Part of our job is to prepare our children for independence and a happy life, a decent life where they can contribute to society. Jacinta thinks such thoughts too, but perhaps her main concern is how society will treat her child.

"There's physical disability and there's mental disability," says Jacinta. "I actually call this social disability. People on the spectrum are not incapable, it's just that they think differently. It's not right or wrong, it's just different, and so the disability they have is their interaction with society, their social interaction."

Another way of framing this is what is known as the 'social model of disability'. As mentioned in an earlier chapter, this model suggests that disability results from the way a society is structured, rather than a person's difference. The neurodiversity movement believes that society should accept autism as just one aspect of humanity. It suggests that society should stop focusing on causes or cures. Rather, the way forward is to help families and individuals lead happier, healthier, productive lives, by providing adequate services and moving away from stigma and negativity.[17]

John Elder Robison, author of such books as *Look Me in the Eye* and *Be Different* advocates for diversity too, but he also believes that individuals on the spectrum may need to change the way they socially interact in order to fit in. I first came across Elder Robison when my mother and mother-in-law attended a talk of his, together, in my hometown of Perth. I was flattered that they'd taken time out to come together and learn more about Asperger's and about their grandson. They were both impressed with Elder Robison's practical approach, and I have to say, it makes sense to me too. Diagnosed with Asperger's as an adult, Elder Robison has taken it upon himself to thoroughly understand his condition and share his insight. After a terribly difficult childhood, he dropped out of school, but soon went on to achieve great success as a sound and light technician, building amplifiers for bands like Kiss and Pink Floyd in the '70s and '80s. Claiming he couldn't talk to humans, yet he could talk to machines, he later ran a successful car repair workshop and it was around this time that he found out about his Asperger's.

He has since become a writer and a warrior for the cause, encouraging people to ponder the blurred line between disability and difference. In an interview on ABC Radio National he enthused:

It has become a passion of mine to go out and speak for the rights of autistic people, to show the rest of the world that we autistics, we are not smarter, we're not better, we're just different, and the rest of the world needs different people. We are a part of diversity...and I see my mission is to go out and spread that word. I think it's an incredible honour, and I would say that we autistics are just coming into our time. We have to stand up and demand the acceptance other groups have achieved.[18]

Elder Robison believes that people on the spectrum need to adapt to social norms in order to survive, and he means that literally. He quotes a disturbing statistic that autistic adults are nine times more likely than neurotypical adults to commit suicide, and attributes this to social isolation and subsequent depression. And he speaks from experience. As a child he struggled to make friends and was constantly misunderstood:

[W]hen I didn't say or do the right things or I didn't respond appropriately, people just thought I was a bad kid, I was selfish, I was self-centred, I was in my own world, I was lazy, I was stupid, and they kind of discarded me. It's only with knowledge of autism that I gained in midlife that I understand the mechanism by which that happened. When I was a little boy I really didn't know any of that. I just knew that kids didn't want to be my friend. I had no idea why.

[A]utistic rights advocates would say that… the world should accommodate you. But…we can only go so far in asking the world to accommodate us. The fact is if our inability to read your body language or your facial expressions causes you to think I'm a callous jerk in the first 10 seconds you meet me, you are never going to know me long enough to decide I'm a nice guy. So it's incumbent upon me to know how to act when I meet you.[19]

I can see where he's coming from. People on the spectrum often have unusual communication styles that can easily be mistaken for rudeness. Unlike physical disabilities, there are often no external markers for autism and because of its invisibility, incidents can, and very often do, get mistaken for bad behaviour. It doesn't matter that lack of eye contact or body awareness is typical for a child on the spectrum. Because in reality people will quickly shut down on a child who is perceived as rude or disrespectful. Even taking too long to process and answer a question can jeopardise chances of forging a friendship. No matter how much we acknowledge that society needs to change—and how much we try and invoke that revolution, the reality is that our kids are living in a judgmental world.

As a mother, it can be extremely painful to see your child misunderstood by their peers, teachers or family members. It is natural to want your child to be liked. But realistically, not everyone is insightful enough to step back and question what has caused an anxiety-filled outburst, rather than taking it personally. Not everyone has access to a bottomless well of patience (not even the most loving of parents on some days!). Jacinta proffers that the key, as a parent, is "not to beat yourself up too much" and to be open with other people about the challenges your child faces. She also suggests that it pays to speak openly with your child about their autism, their strengths and weaknesses, so they can build their self-awareness.

"I've always been honest and just called it for what it is," says Jacinta. "People have said 'have you told him about his diagnosis?' to which I reply 'well, you can hardly take him to all these doctors and therapists and not tell him what it's all about'. He's only ever tried to use it as a crutch once and I pulled him up very quickly and went 'no way, you're not doing that'. I said to him 'don't you ever tell me or somebody else that you can't do something because you're autistic', so that stopped very quickly. He certainly can't use it as an excuse.

"Being honest with him helps him to understand and hopefully feel a little less frustrated. I also try to be open with other parents and I find that 90 to 95 per cent of parents that you talk to understand. Sometimes things will be travelling along nicely, he'll be polite and compliant and then the wheels fall off and they sort of look at you as if to say 'what just happened?' I'll say, 'I'm sorry, I had no idea why he just hit your child, but I'll try and find out'.

"Of course it's impossible to keep on top of every little incident. It can be worrying when a parent approaches you in the playground. You're never really sure whether they want to talk to you about something good or not so good. It can be stressful going to the school, or getting a phone call from the school. You're never quite sure what it's going to be about. It might be something innocent, but life is tense because your heart is bleeding for the different things that happen to your child during the day."

Another tip Jacinta suggests is to get involved with the school. As well as volunteering to help with the usual fundraising fetes and trivia nights, Jacinta has assisted the school in lodging funding applications. She finds it is a good way to get to know the teachers and how the system works. I too have always been involved with my children's school, helping children who have difficulty reading, and serving sandwiches in the canteen. Now I'm involved with P&C at their high school, where students have not one teacher, but many—where they are not one of a small community, but a much bigger one.

"If you want the best for your child you have to be willing to put the time and effort in and show that you are available to work with the school," says Jacinta. "They also find it very difficult to reprimand your child if you're always volunteering at the school. While you're at it, be an advocate for your child. It's also a good way to hear about what's happening, to find out some truths or half-truths.

"One of the things that we've always done is in the first week of any new class, we go and meet the teacher, give them our business cards and say 'these are our contact details and we want to hear it from you, not the grapevine.' We tell them 'these are our rules at home, our reward systems, and you can take those on or do your own thing. The important thing is we want to work with you and support you. We are not parents who think our child is an angel. He can be an angel, but can also be the devil incarnate.' Showing a willingness to be open with teachers can go a long way."

It is a luxury that Elder Robison and many other undiagnosed children never experienced. Even today, even with family support and teacher awareness, school can be a tough place to be for a kid on the spectrum. Until they can make their mark in the world and specialise in a skill, they will continue to come up against obstacles and quite often fail. Elder Robison believes this is what separates disability from difference. He writes: "If you're eccentric or even weird, but you're not failing at work or in your personal life, you are not disabled. You're just different. It's only when you fail at some key thing—as I did—that you become 'officially' disabled."[20]

For him, the breakthrough came when he started his career in sound and lighting on the rock band circuit, and again when he became a car mechanic. By acquiring specialist skills he garnered respect and a place in the world. He refers to this leap forward as proof of the 'competence-deviance hypothesis', which suggests that the more competence a person has, the more people tolerate their difference or deviance from the norm. While this might work for an adult in an established career, it is difficult for a child who is yet to prove themselves to the world—for a child who struggles at school and who might be perceived as having 'behavioural issues', as being rude or lazy.

Elder Robison writes:

> In my experience, that is the path from disabled to gifted. You learn social skills. You find life and work in settings that minimise your weaknesses, and you discover your strengths and play to them. It sounds easy, set out like that but it entails a huge amount of work. It's been a life-time job for me, but the results are worth it all.[21]

Zac, like many kids on the spectrum, has strengths beyond his years—strengths that will no doubt hold him in good stead in the future, but as Jacinta says, "we have a way to go yet".

"I see Zac and I am amazed at some of the things he can do," she says. "I still marvel at his attention to detail, and his memory retention is unbelievable. But his toolbox of executive management skills is empty. You give him something to do and he'll just stare at it because he doesn't know where to start. It's a matter of getting him started and getting him engaged. Once he's engaged, once he's started, he's fine. As with most things, he needs a bit of a nudge, but he gets there in the end."

Secret garden

Anna, George & Cassie

I pull up outside a 1950s weatherboard cottage with neatly edged lawns. The house stands apart from the other cookie-cutter homes on the street because of its established garden, in which an incongruous mix of prickly cacti and succulents straddle sweet-smelling jasmine, pink camellias and red geraniums. While this garden is a lush, suburban oasis, the other yards in this South-Western Sydney street are mostly comprised of parched, plain-looking lawn.

I am here to interview Anna and George, and their daughter Cassie, who lives in a granny flat out the back. It is the first day of summer and already the air conditioners in this part of town are buzzing for lack of a sea breeze. Anna and George don't own an air conditioner, but a huge gum tree in the backyard shades the house.

George greets me at the door. "You found the place OK then?" he asks and guides me to the lounge room where Anna is waiting. It is difficult to place her age, but the grey curls framing her face suggest she is in her 60s.

"Thanks for coming. Have a seat," Anna says and motions to a comfy-looking armchair. I move a crocheted rug to one side and am immediately reminded of my grandmother's lounge room, with its springy armchairs and vases of randomly arranged blossoms, the aroma of cheese biscuits, and cricket on the television. Much like this place, Grandma's living room was spotless, with everything in its place, yet cosy and welcoming.

"Cup of tea?" asks George. "Coffee? We have green tea or peppermint," he offers.

"Just a glass of water would be lovely," I reply. I look around. Cacti in small coloured pots line the kitchen windowsill. An embroidered tablecloth pretties up the dining table. Christmas cards hang on a length of string across an arched doorway, and it strikes me that Anna and George are of a generation that still sends greeting cards, rather than posting an impersonal message on social media.

Moments later Anna is telling me her story. She and George met in the early 1970s at their local Friday night church youth group. She was 16 and he was 18 and they were both living with their families, not far from where we now sit.

"You had to be 16 to go to CYO (Catholic Youth Organisation)," explains Anna. "It was where you went to meet a good Catholic boy and the only place I was allowed to go by myself."

One year later, the couple became engaged, but not before Anna's parents interrogated George over Sunday lunch, the ultimate challenge for a quiet young man who had never excelled in the art of conversation.

"I remember her parents kept asking me questions," says George. "I'd be talking and they'd be eating, just watching me, and I wasn't sure when to talk or when to stop. I guess it went alright though. I'm still here to tell the story and her father is a good friend."

They married when Anna was 20 and bought the house in which they now live. George was employed as an apprentice for a large telecommunications company, where he loyally remained for 41 years until his recent retrenchment. He now describes himself as "the house-husband and support crew". Anna, meanwhile, completed a Diploma of Teaching and worked as a primary school teacher. After several stressful years of trying to fall pregnant and a number of miscarriages, she gave birth to their first daughter, Gillian. "I was 26 when I had Gillian. I thought I was ancient," Anna remarks. Four years later she had their second daughter, Cassie. These days Anna works as a tutor from the kitchen table adjacent to where we are sitting.

A smiling young woman wearing a black t-shirt and black jeans suddenly appears and hands me a glass of icy water. "I thought you were the postie," she enthuses. "I'm expecting some seeds to arrive in the mail."

"This is Cassie," says Anna. "She loves gardening as much as George and I do."

On the front of Cassie's t-shirt is a picture of Chewbacca. Cassie has an urban, geeky look that would fit right in at my local inner city second-hand bookstore, but her style is slightly out of kilter with this home's traditional aesthetic.

"My garden is out the back," beams Cassie. "You should come and see it. I like growing things from seed. It's difficult, but interesting. I started gardening when I was four. I entered competitions and won. Actually, I entered a lot of competitions—writing, design, art competitions. I won a lot of things. Sorry, stop me if I talk too much," she adds with sincerity.

We all smile. I later regret not accepting Cassie's invitation to see her garden near the granny flat. I'm curious to know what species she has planted and see how she has nurtured them to life. But by the end of the interview I feel that I have already asked too much of this family. They have been overly generous with their time and conversation and I politely leave through the front door. Cassie's secret garden is left to my imagination.

Cassie, who is 35, was diagnosed with ADHD at the age of seven and Asperger's at age 11. It was the late 1990s, not long after Asperger's became formerly recognised and when very few people knew or understood what Asperger's meant, particularly for girls. At the time, Anna happened to be working as a secretary for a learning difficulties organisation. She had essentially assumed the role to do a friend a favour. "I went to their offices and picked up a pamphlet that stated 'is your child inflexible, and socially inept?' There was a litany of my children's and George's foibles. I then got online because we had just got the internet and that opened up a lot of doors to the information I was seeking."

Cassie's diagnosis actually came shortly after her sister Gillian's, who was in Year 8 at the time. "The teachers kept saying that Gillian was well behaved and she was bright, but she would come home and fly into a terrible rage and cry for hours," says Anna. "She was big on structure. She would get terribly anxious if the maths teacher was away, for example. They'd sit the kids on the netball court for supervision, which the other kids thought was the best thing ever, but for her it was disastrous because there was no structure. And she'd let the other kids know, which went down like a lead balloon. She'd wear school uniform on mufti day. She couldn't cope with change.

"On one occasion she was left behind at a school athletics carnival. She didn't notice five coaches of kids leaving and even scarier, the teacher didn't notice that she was missing. That's when I said to George, 'I think we're in deep shit'. And when I started looking at Asperger's."

As well as not coping with the school environment, Gillian was being bullied every day. Anna tried for years to move her to a different school, but none of the local public schools would allow it because the family was out of area. "I didn't know what to do. I should have pulled her out and homeschooled her.[22] But I was worried it would disadvantage her. I was worried I couldn't do the work and I thought high school would be a good place for her because she was bright. She wanted to be a scientist. I was just so undecided and I just kept thinking it would get better. I would be at the school two, three times a week. It was a terribly stressful time."

Things did improve when Gillian was accepted into a selective school for Years 11 and 12, and was joined at the school by her younger sister. Gillian now lives in Adelaide and works as a scientist, as she'd planned, but she declined to be interviewed for this book. She explains through emails to her mother that she wants to get on with her career without dwelling on her diagnosis. She also doesn't want to relive the trauma of her school years.

Cassie, on the other hand, is happy to speak about her experiences. She was diagnosed with Asperger's when she was still in primary school and her school years were far less traumatic than her sister's. Before long Cassie is telling me about her interest in fan fiction, a form of creative writing that involves reimagining television series and movies. It was through this that she met her best friend Shirley, whom she eventually visited in Canada.

"We met online and I saved up to go and see her in Vancouver a couple of years ago," says Cassie. "We're both keen creative writers, except I also create entire worlds and maps and cultures as well. I can spend hours and hours doing a single map.

"Shirley wrote all these wonderful reviews about my stories that I put online and then she became the editor for one particular story. It was a remake of an anime TV series, a much darker version. She loved it and through that we became really good friends."

I sense that Cassie could talk about her love of writing for some time, although she later tells me she hasn't always been so enthusiastic about the written word, struggling to read and write until about the age of 10.

"I didn't have an interest in reading when I was little," she explains. "I found it really hard and boring, but when I started writing creatively, I actually started doing a lot more reading. And now

I'm very good at writing and I'm better than Mum at editing. The fact that I'm a fast typer helps."

Cassie was a challenging and defiant child, according to Anna. She would run away and take herself to the shops at age two and catch a train to the city by herself at age nine. She was identified as having a high IQ when tested at seven, yet Anna explains that she did not have the emotional intelligence to match. "While part of her intellect was at age 15 or 16, her comprehension and EQ was at age five," says Anna.

Anna worried that people might take advantage of Cassie because of her immaturity. In fact, she still worries about this and was terribly anxious when Cassie visited Shirley in Canada. "We were pretty beside ourselves when Cassie took herself off to meet a complete stranger on the other side of the world. I made her swear she would text me every day and told her that if I didn't receive a text I would call the police—and I meant it. She slept under a bridge and stayed with people she didn't know and did a whole lot of things that I was terrified about, but thankfully Shirley didn't turn out to be an axe murderer or anything. Quite the opposite."

Today, Cassie strikes me as a capable, bubbly conversationalist. She also boasts three university degrees—a Bachelor and Masters of Science in Environmental Earth Science and a Masters of Primary Teaching. She took up the teaching qualification when she couldn't get work in science, and now, like her mum, works from home as a tutor.

"I couldn't get into the workplace because I don't interview well," she says.

"You're doing pretty well so far," I joke, referring to our current conversation, but I know that a formal job interview would be a more intimidating setting.

"I never know what people want me to say and when to say it. Do they want me to fill in the quiet spaces? Should I stop talking? Because I know I talk too much. I have no ability of knowing when to say something in a conversation, because you wait for people to pause and I never know the right moment to start talking. And I don't want to say something that is wrong or off-putting or distracting or horrible. Everyone else seems to know how to do it.

"I'm not a social person. I don't have friends. I don't need friends. I'm friendly with my students' parents, and I go out with my family. That's enough."

I look to George, sitting next to Cassie on the couch. A self-confessed "wallflower", he smiles and nods. "We're quite similar in many ways, but also very different," he says, quietly. Cassie concurs.

"Sometimes when Mum goes on holidays she leaves us a list," says Cassie. "Dad and I will just stare at it and say to each other 'what exactly does she mean by that?' We're both very literal, whereas Mum isn't. I say to her, 'you need to be very specific with your instructions'. Dad and I also don't like surprises. We need to know what is happening a long way in advance. I do think Dad understands me in some ways better than Mum."

George was diagnosed with ADHD when Anna insisted he visit a psychologist not long after the girls with diagnosed. He took stimulant medication for some time, which he said helped him to focus better and not get as easily distracted. But on the whole, he said the diagnosis did little to change anything for him, perhaps because it came so late in life.

Like Cassie, George had difficulty with reading as a child, which he suspects was dyslexia. He disliked school and used to run away when things became too tough. These were in the days when teachers were big on punitive measures, including the cane.

"I'd just collect my bag in the break and take off," George explains. "I remember once being hit by the teacher for every spelling mistake and I got 37 wrong out of 50. I then ran home and then got a belting from my mother for absconding."

Not surprisingly, these tactics failed to improve his scores. In Year Eight, however, his parents had him IQ tested. He was subsequently moved from the D class to the middle of the B class, which greatly improved his self-esteem. I am reminded of Ross W. Greene's philosophy that poor motivation is an "overrated, over invoked explanation for why children do not meet our expectations". He writes, "The vast majority of children do not get their jollies by making themselves and those around them miserable."[23] Rather than punishing a child for what they can't do, supporting them with their difficulties and nurturing their strengths can empower and encourage them. Perhaps this is why George went on to finish school and find his niche in life.

George's approach to life is a systematic one, no doubt useful in his chosen field of telecommunications. Anna speaks of the time that George "lost it" when she left a folded up brochure in his wallet. Mother's Day was coming up and she had rather unsubtly circled a potential gift idea on the brochure. But George was not impressed, for his wallet was where he methodically kept his money and credit cards, and he let the family know. He had what Cassie describes as a "full-blown meltdown". "His meltdowns are very rare," says Cassie. "But they kind of freak you out when they do happen." It was a matter of George having his system and Anna messing with it.

But it strikes me that Anna has her systems and expectations too. She comes across as stern and conventional in many ways, largely motivated by a burning desire to help and understand her family. As such, she has an insatiable thirst for information and has spent many hours researching and trying to work out how her husband and daughters operate. In this, she reminds me of myself.

"I don't actually think the diagnoses changed anything for them," says Anna. "But it made a huge difference for me. It helped me to understand how they worked and how I could help."

Her statement stays with me. Are diagnoses just a way for neurotypicals to come to grips with differently wired individuals? I ponder how Tom's life might have looked had he not been diagnosed. Would I have understood him any less? Would his teachers and relatives have understood him any less? Would he have a different perspective? In our case, I think a diagnosis has been immensely beneficial. I like to think that it has helped to make his life more rewarding.

George, however, can't see what all the fuss is about.

"I have always just taken the girls as they are," says George. "I would try and understand and do the right thing as a parent, but it was usually the opposite to how Anna wanted it to be. I couldn't seem to do it right, so I just went back to being myself.

"Anna would be frustrated and mad and cranky at me for not doing something a particular way, or disciplining the girls. We'd go off on different tangents for a while, but we tried to keep communicating, to keep talking about it.

"Sometimes my way works best. Like when Cassie was little and wouldn't read and I told her we'd buy her the little Star Trek books if she'd look at them. I'm not sure she technically read them, but she looked at them."

This is all very close to the bone. I think of the way I berate James when he makes silly 'Dad jokes' and I tell him Tom doesn't always understand sarcasm. Or when he doesn't monitor the kids' screen time like I do. Or when he steps in and does the kids' chores for them, because it's easier than having to confront them. His sometimes blasé approach to parenting drives me to distraction, but I also recognise that I need to loosen up. And sometimes his way does work best.

"George never disciplined the girls," says Anna. "He's lucky that they were pretty good and not into drugs or anything. If they were taking ice he'd probably just say 'maybe you shouldn't take quite so much ice.' But I have to say, he's always been there for them."

Like most couples, George and Anna have had their ups and downs, no doubt amplified by the pressure of having two daughters with additional needs, while "trying to juggle work and life in general" as Anna puts it.

For Anna, the juggle has invariably taken its toll. She has had two nervous breakdowns and has been on antidepressants for 15 years, which "helps keep the lid on". She doesn't want to say it in front of Cassie, but she was close to leaving the family several times.

"I knew that if I left, the kids would not benefit by that at all, so I made the decision to stay, which in hindsight was the right decision. But it was hard, very hard. Especially when Gillian was being bullied every day for two and a half years. And then I thought it would get easier, but then it was HSC and then it was uni and then they needed to get a job. Sometimes it doesn't feel like there is an end in sight."

Tears are rolling down Anna's cheeks. I feel like I want to reach over and hug her, but I fear she wouldn't appreciate it. It is probably not very professional of me. Besides, Anna strikes me as a pragmatic woman, no-nonsense and sensible to a fault. Perhaps this is a demeanour she has established in order to cope. I suspect that underneath her stern, tenacious exterior she is an exhausted, fragile heap. I wholeheartedly empathise with Anna and am all too familiar with the mental load that mothers take on board, the constant organisation of home and family that men do not seem to burden themselves with.[24]

Anna cites the statistic that 90 per cent of marriages end in divorce when there is a child with autism, a statistic I have heard before. Barry M. Prizant, however, disputes the "perennial myth that three out of four marriages that produce a child with autism end in divorce." He writes: "There is no reliable research to back up that claim. In any case, about half of all marriages in the United States end in divorce. Is the rate higher when autism is a factor? Nobody knows for sure." He writes that what we do know is that "Raising a child with a disability can be stressful. If there are already cracks in the foundation of a marriage, then having a child with autism adds additional pressure, and that could lead to divorce."[25] He also adds that in some cases, divorce or separation is not necessarily a bad thing and can ultimately benefit the whole family. Nevertheless, Anna says she has witnessed several real-life cases, in her support group, where it's been all too much and divorce is the only way out.

"I think a lot of women cut their husbands loose because they don't have the emotional power to be doing all that heavy lifting with two people. You can't function with a partner who is not pulling their weight when you've got a 24/7 kid. I've seen it play out in the support groups I used to go to."

There have been many times when Anna and George's parenting decisions have clashed. One of the most memorable for Anna was when she told Cassie, then 24, that she needed to move out of home. Anna had a grand plan that involved both daughters working full time and living out of home by the time they were 25 and Cassie was fast approaching her deadline. George, on the other hand, was more relaxed about this grand plan.

"That's when George and I had our last big argument," Anna says. "I asked Cassie to leave home and George said 'no, you can stay here'. I said 'not at 24, 34 and 44. What are you thinking?' Cassie was living the life of Riley."

Anna had laid down the rules early on, when each of the girls finished school: "We would pay for their first degree and for their Masters. I was working two jobs to get them through uni, and George was working full time. I said 'after that the gravy train finishes and you're on your own. I will give you 12 months of saving up to get some money behind you and then you're out of here'. I had it all worked out and it certainly didn't involve having eternal students living at home with us forever and a day."

Gillian moved to Adelaide at the age of 24 and eventually, by the age of 30, saved enough to buy her own house. Cassie, much to Anna's chagrin, continued studying.

"George came home and said 'well that's done. I've pre-enrolled Cassie in a Masters of Teaching. We've paid the money, it's all done'," says Anna.

"I said, 'are you joking?' Neither of them had spoken to me about it and I was furious because that was not the agreement we'd made. I didn't want her doing three degrees and living here and not working."

At that moment, Cassie interrupts and explains that she actually paid for her Masters of Teaching degree, not her parents. She saved her money by delivering thousands of newspapers and brochures over several years. Then, after completing her teaching studies she took up tutoring work, but was still only working 10 hours a week and living at home.

"George and I were both working full time and I thought, this can't go on. In some ways it was to my disadvantage to ask her to leave because she was very useful. I'd ask her to unpack the dishwasher, bring the washing in et cetera and she knew not to say no. But I could see the future coming and I thought 'no, I want to lie on the lounge. I'd love to work 10 hours a week!' So I gave her a date and said 'you need to move out by this date'."

Cassie scoured the classifieds and found an advertisement for a room in a sharehouse nearby, very nearby.

"I was gobsmacked," says Anna. "I thought she'd say, 'you're pissing me off, I'm moving to Uluru' and I would have said 'fine, go!' Instead, she opts to live, literally within sightline of our home, so obviously I didn't push her too hard."

Cassie regularly popped in for dinner and called on George to help with maintenance. One evening she called on him at 11 pm to catch a Huntsman spider in her bedroom. On a few occasions he changed a light bulb for her. But Cassie was not happy with the new living arrangement and moved into a flat three blocks from home. Meanwhile, inheritances from George and Anna's mothers gave them the final cash injection they needed to build Cassie a flat in the backyard.

"We had thought about it for a while but could never afford it," explains Anna. "In hindsight, building the flat is the best decision we have ever made. We have dual frontage, so Cassie has her own driveway, her own entrance and her own garden. It also gives Gillian a place to live should she choose to return from Adelaide. We hope to move in there when we are 80 and swap. It will also give the girls an income stream when we're gone."

In some ways, Anna and George have the best of both worlds. They get to enjoy their daughter's company, but also lead a life of their own. They regularly see Cassie, but enjoy a certain amount of privacy. Cassie has independence and contributes to the family finances, while they have their couch back.

Cassie is undoubtedly happy with the arrangement, but she is also aware that she hasn't met her mother's expectations. "I am working 30 hours a week as a tutor. I'm technically money solvent. I pay Mum and Dad rent, I pay my medical insurance, I pay my car insurance. But I know that it upsets Mum that I can't get full-time employment."

Anna later tells me that everyone in the family tree has worked. "We don't breed couch potatoes," she explains. "And for a while there, Cassie was a couch potato."

I catch myself pondering what my own situation might look like in years to come. The thought of having adult children living at home is confronting, because so much of what we do as parents is to ready our children for the day they will finally leave home and a start a life of their own. And I am the first to admit, I often dream of the day that James and I will finally have time to ourselves. Like Anna, I have always presumed that my children would find their own way, leaving James and me to grow old together. But my mind is racing back and forth between the past, the present and to the future. Tom has nowhere near the life skills I had at his age. Neither does he have the drive or motivation that I had. I moved out of home when I was 18. Studying at university, I also worked three part-time jobs to pay the rent, to maintain a clapped-out Fiat and to feed and water myself. Add to this the fact that we live in a city where rents and mortgages are ridiculously unaffordable for young people, and my children's narrative is looking a little different to mine.

As I listen to the banter back and forth between the three people on the couch before me, I see a close-knit family unit that enjoys each other's company, and that is reassuring. Some parents hardly ever see their adult children, yet Cassie and her parents socialise together. She recently joined George and Anna's gardening club. While considerably younger than the other group members, she has plenty in common with them and Anna tells me they "love her to bits".

"You could have pushed me over with a feather when she said she was coming to Gardening Club," says Anna. "I wasn't sure how it was going to go, Cassie being Cassie. But she has a real passion for it and she fits right in."

I comment on how close the family seems, what a wonderful unit they are, how lucky they are to have each other. But Anna feels the wrench of Cassie and Gillian's limited social circle. "I'd give it all up, all of that, for one friend for them. One friend. Someone who loves them as much as I do."

Anna says she worked out pretty early on that she and George "were it". "I don't remember seeing them with other friends past about the age of 15 or 16, around the time other teenagers started going to parties and having boyfriends. The girls never had a sleepover and very few birthday invitations. It didn't take me long to work out that our family unit was their social network. And there were no social skills classes at the time.

"People don't quite get what I mean when I say to people that the girls don't go out. They think I mean that they've got three friends, or a boyfriend. I think without exception, my girlfriends' children of a similar age are in romantic relationships. Maybe a few of them are single, but they have dated and they go out with friends. But our girls really have no one they can turn to. They are 100 per cent emotionally dependent on us.

"Gillian was diagnosed with meningitis a few weeks ago and I was panic-stricken. I thought 'what happens if she's sick in the middle of the night'? She's in Adelaide, I'm in Sydney. There's no one she can turn to. What will happen when I'm gone?"

By this stage Anna is crying again, and so am I, because I get it. It sounds gloomy, but I quite often wonder who would help Tom if something were to happen to me. No one else knows about his routine, about his medication, his therapy, his tutoring, his executive function difficulties. More than that, no one else gets him the way I do. I sense that Anna shares a similar sense of responsibility, even though her daughters are adults.

"I've talked to the girls about freezing their eggs," says Anna, choking back more tears. "I said I'd be supportive of whatever they chose to do, but they have both said no because of their autism. They don't want to pass it on, and I hold myself accountable for that because I've never lied to them and I wonder if I've painted too dark a picture of the difficulties, for their own protection. Being girls, they were very open to being abused by people. Particularly Cassie was so immature until about 24 or so. But perhaps I made a mistake by being too honest."

I'm not entirely sure what she means by this. I'm gathering that she means she has discouraged the girls from having an intimate relationship because they might be taken advantage of. And now she is regretful and sad about that.

George, the 'support crew', hands both Anna and me a tissue. A slight smile reveals his gentle disposition. He is a sweet man and I sense there have been very many tissues before now. Anna has worked so hard to help her daughters to become independent, successful young adults. She goes on to tell me about the time she took the school to tribunal, and the time she took on Centrelink, and won both cases. At the start of each year, she would ring every teacher to discuss the girls' needs. Being a teacher she understood the system better than some.

"Gillian wanted to be a scientist when she was six years old. Cassie made that decision when she was four. I told them I'd never stand in their way. I wanted what they wanted."

It is clear that Anna has done everything within her power to get the girls through school and help them to carve out a career. George has contributed enormously too, including the time he held a Vice-Chancellor to account when Gillian failed her Bachelor degree because the university had lost her exam paper. George sat outside the Vice-Chancellor's office and told his staff that he would not leave until the issue was resolved.

"George printed out the faculty handbook, all 54 pages of it," says Anna. "I was working so I said 'take this, go to the uni and don't leave until it's sorted.' He did, he got it sorted. For a man who is dyslexic, that was huge.

"I told him to make them search the office until they found her exam paper. They found it of course and quickly offered her the scholarship she applied for, but I told her not to take it because it was hush money. I then went on to write 27 letters to every part of the chain that let her down. We did it though. We got both girls through the system."

Like the cacti amongst the soft pink camellias and scented jasmine, this family arrangement is incongruous, but it seems to work. It functions as a whole unit, each individual species unique in its own right, each complementing the exceptional qualities of the other. The arrangement may not be what Anna or George had in mind. But they have adapted, and even the most rare species have found a place to flourish, grown from seed. They have something grander than a neatly edged lawn. They have a secret garden thriving in their very own backyard.

Dolls in the closet

Juliet & Gabriel

Her dark hair is tied back in a loose ponytail, stray strands falling around her face. She is wearing bright red lipstick and a necklace of beads the same shade. Her name is Juliet, she is mother to Gabriel, aged 18. And when she speaks, I listen. I hang on her every word, for Juliet exudes a certain intensity. It is an intensity that I recognise in myself to some degree, a seriousness that I have developed since having children, along with grey hair and a lined brow. But in Juliet, this intensity manifests as a strength, a magnetism. She speaks with deep concentration and articulation, devoid of the girlish giggles or silly jokes I'm prone to make in order to fill in the blank spaces.

We meet in a busy inner Melbourne café, but the clinking of cutlery, cheery conversation and loud music is too distracting. I need to concentrate on Juliet's words and I want to allow her the opportunity to speak her mind. She has, after all, taken time out of her day, her busy life, to meet with me and to share her story—that is, the story of her life with Gabriel. When Juliet speaks of Gabriel, she glows with pride. She describes a sensitive boy with a sharp sense of humour. She describes Gabriel's resilience after being teased at school and how now, after some fairly challenging years, he is pursuing a passion for hairdressing. She also hints at their close relationship. Juliet is a single mother and it is clear she has dedicated the past 18 years to Gabriel's happiness. But she is also an artist, an avid gardener and, not coincidentally, a passionate autism advocate.

Escaping the noise of the café, Juliet and I adjourn to a nearby library and find a quiet corner in the Young Adult Literature section, surrounded by graphic novels and tales of vampires. There I start my tape recorder rolling and as Juliet speaks I start to get an insight into her life experience, extending back to her Latin heritage. Juliet's parents were among the masses of refugees who fled Spain to escape the wrath of the merciless Nationalist leader Francisco Franco, following the Spanish Civil War. When Franco won the war in 1939 there were harsh reprisals for his Republican enemies. Hundreds of thousands of people were executed and many more were used for slave labour, building railways and roads, and digging canals. Escaping the terror in their home country, Juliet's parents migrated to Venezuela, where Juliet was born and spent the first five years of her life, together with her brother. But while Venezuela was a good place to live in the 1950s, the political instability of the '60s forced Juliet's parents to move again, this time to Australia. Juliet remembers her childhood in Melbourne as difficult but spirited. Neither she nor her parents knew English when they arrived, but there was always humour to fall back on. She remembers her father, a cartoonist, drawing caricatures of other migrants with their black socks on at the beach, carrying "everything but the kitchen sink". Juliet learnt early on in life that despite hardship, there was always something to smile about, a trait that has remained with her as a parent and one she believes she has passed down to Gabriel.

When Gabriel was diagnosed with Asperger's at the age of seven, she says it was her sense of humour and the entrenched resilience of being a migrant that allowed her to cope. This was in the early 2000s. Like many people then, all Juliet knew about autism was from the film *Rain Man*. Around the time of Gabriel's diagnosis, Juliet's brother died, and subsequently her mother fell into deep depression. Her GP refused to label or treat the depression, which didn't help, and Juliet's husband refused to acknowledge their son's autism. The marriage soon ended and

Juliet's husband moved out. While still in communi-cation with Juliet and Gabriel, he has since played less of a hands-on role in parenting.

"He was convinced I'd organised this diagnosis, rather than it being an outcome of me just looking for answers," she explains. Interestingly, she now thinks that many of her husband's traits could in fact be la-beled autistic. I reflect on this and wonder what parent of a child on the spectrum hasn't had that thought about their partner or indeed, themselves? James and I often remark to each other: "That's the Aspie in you," only half-jokingly. Yesterday, for example, I found James watching an historical documentary on trains. Hospital trains of World War I to be precise. He was glued, and it looked more than a little like hyperfocus!

Despite our individual quirks and regular disagree-ments, James and I have always been on the same page with Tom's diagnosis. Granted, there are times I have wished James would be a little more involved, or read the books I've handed to him—the ones marked with the post-it notes saying 'READ THIS!' in capital let-ters. But on the whole we've always agreed that the diagnosis is spot-on and had a similar vision about how to move forward. I've come across numerous parents who have not been so fortunate, which either means one parent—usually the mother—ends up pick-ing up all of the slack when it comes to liaising with the school and therapy, or, perhaps inevitably, the relationship dissolves. Having a child on the spectrum is hard work (as is having a neurotypical child). But I imagine it would be even harder if one parent were in denial about the diagnosis.

Juliet's search for answers was prompted by a series of incidents at Gabriel's school. He was struggling to fit in and was quickly attracting the label of a 'naughty boy' from the teachers. Halfway through the kindergarten year, the teacher approached Juliet in the playground at pick-up time and blurted out: "Is he pulling my leg or does he have a problem?"

Juliet recalls: "She didn't choose to make an appointment, or speak to me earlier in the year about his behaviour, or take me aside to a private place to go through some of the behaviours she was observing."

As it turned out, Gabriel was getting distracted in class and not sitting still when he was supposed to. Schools now recognise that moving about in a classroom, or sitting on a fitness ball instead of a chair, or having regular breaks outdoors, for instance, can help children with focus, productivity and behaviour. But there was none of this for Gabriel. He was also struggling with social interactions in the classroom and wasn't making friends. On one occasion he cut another little girl's t-shirt and Juliet was told she had to replace it.

"The incident was not deconstructed and contextualised," Juliet reflects. "I was told he was 'naughty', 'way out of control' and 'the only way he is going to learn is if we make you pay [for the t-shirt]'. When I spoke to the other mother she said she didn't think it was necessary, but the teacher insisted we bring in another shirt we'd already bought."

At another time, the children were invited to bring along their favourite toys for playtime. Gabriel chose to bring along his favourite dolls, namely ones with long hair. In hindsight, Juliet now realises it was all about the hair. He taught himself to plait hair on those dolls and would draw designs of hairstyles—a fascination which has now grown into the beginnings of a hairdressing career. Back then, however, Juliet just thought Gabriel loved dolls and encouraged him to pursue his passion. Unfortunately the school had other thoughts. The dolls had prompted some teasing from other children and Juliet received a phone call from the principal.

"I'm called up to the office with the principal and the counsellor and I'm told, these were the exact words, I'll never forget them, 'Get Gabriel to tone down his interest in dolls and he won't get bullied'. My response to that was 'so he, who is the victim, is punished, but the perpetrators are not.' And I said very, very clearly in that meeting, to this very persistent counsellor: 'Forget it. I will not limit him. I'm not going to have my child play in a cupboard with his dolls.'"

Juliet says it wasn't just schoolteachers who questioned her judgment and Gabriel's supposed gender attraction, but other parents gave her a hard time too. In the end she won out and continued to encourage Gabriel to bring his dolls to school, but the issue divided the school community. This was 2006. It's hard to believe that this would happen now, when schools have 'wear it purple day' in support of same-sex attraction and rainbow kids. But even in my fairly liberated inner Sydney locale, I've heard of children being teased still for their same-sex preference.

Also, despite my supposed open-mindedness, I have a confession to make. When Juliet told me she encouraged her son to play with dolls at school, a part of me thought 'Why would you do that? Aren't you just setting him up to be a target for bullies?' And this is where I am a big chicken and perhaps a little bit of a social desperado. I have always encouraged Tom to pursue interests that the other kids at school pursue. Granted, he's found many of them (specifically, any sport or any popular fad) dead boring, and fair enough. But thankfully he has had enough interest in all things dinosaurs, Star Wars and Minecraft to carry out conversations that could ultimately lead to friendships. I work hard to make social interactions easier for him and not more challenging than they need to be. It's not to say I don't champion difference and diversity, but I also have a paradoxical desire for my own child to fit in. We've been fortunate that Tom's special interests in countries and cultures, architecture and art are socially acceptable—that he doesn't have a special interest in such random delights as wing nuts, or rare diseases, or that stereotypical Aspie favourite, train timetables. If he did have an interest in dolls, like Gabriel, I actually don't know if I'd try and steer him away from it or not. After all, therapists say that for a child on the spectrum to thrive, it's important to allow them time to focus on their special interest. And indeed this is why Aspies make the best experts, because they have an uncanny ability to focus on their interest and can often quickly surpass their parent's knowledge of that topic.

Barry M. Prizant refers to these interests as "enthusiasms", adopted from Clara Claiborne Park, who wrote the groundbreaking memoir on autism called *The Siege* back in 1967. Prizant writes:

> Children with autism develop all kinds of enthusiasms, talking nonstop about or focusing endlessly on subjects like skyscrapers, animal species, geography, particular kinds of music, sunrise and sunset times, or turnpike exits. Perhaps focusing on one topic gives the child a sense of control, of predictability and security in a world that can be unpredictable and feel scary.[26]

Prizant describes how, just as anyone might take comfort in a hobby, an "enthusiasm" or special interest "feeds a basic neurological need to be engaged, to appreciate beauty, and to experience positive emotion."[27] In other words, a special interest can be emotionally soothing for an autistic child—and it can actually help parents and teachers in dealing with behavioural issues.

If Gabriel's teacher was sufficiently trained in special needs and knew that he was autistic, she could have used his dolls as a reward or soother for those times when he was feeling stressed. She could have also used them to demonstrate to other children that toys are not necessarily gender-specific, benefiting the other children and in turn society, but I suppose she'd then have a few parents to contend with. Tony Attwood writes:

> The [special] interest can be either a barrier or bridge to social contact, but can also be used constructively at school and in psychological therapies or become the basis of a successful career. When one considers the attributes associated with the special interests, it is important to consider not only the benefits to the person with Asperger's syndrome, but also the benefits to society.[28]

Even Hans Asperger himself considered that a successful scientist or artist needed "a dash of autism" and the ability to "turn away from the everyday world, from the simply practical…to re-think a subject with originality so as to create in new untrodden ways, with all abilities canalised into the one specialty".[29] If Gabriel wasn't allowed the opportunity to plait the hair of his dolls, he may never have found his chosen profession nor would he be quite so happy as he is now.

Despite my own somewhat cowardly approach toward encouraging 'schoolyard friendly' special interests, I hold enormous respect for people like Juliet who have the courage to buck the system. After all, why should our children have to conform to what the powers-that-be think is normal or right? Standing up for difference and challenging stereotypes in the schoolyard shows the next generation of thinkers that bullying is not acceptable—be it persecution because of sexual preference, gender, race or ability. In *Not Even Wrong: Adventures in Autism*, Paul Collins writes that "Autists are ultimate square pegs, and the problem with pounding a square peg into a round hole is not that the hammering is hard work. It's that you're destroying the peg".[30] As I write this, the world is mourning the death of David Bowie, the ultimate creative spirit. Even in his final days he used his creativity to narrate and explore his fate through music and film. Social media outlets have gone into overdrive about Bowie—musician, showman, designer, gentlemanly activist whose 'other-worldliness' paved the way for other people to express their originality. Thank goodness for Bowie and other square pegs.

That said, as a parent I feel responsible for making my child's experience of living in a round-hole world much easier. I remember early on in the piece, one therapist suggested that parents need to prepare their child for the big, bad world where the simple act of going to the gym, for example, with all of its loud music, bright lights and sweaty bodies, could be a sensory nightmare (personally, I hate gyms for that very reason, but I'd like to allow my son to the opportunity to make his own decision). In response to Collins, Joel Yanofsky writes in *Bad Animals*: "What's wrong, for instance, with trying to smooth out the square peg just a bit before you start hammering it into the round hole?"[31] In other words, why not give autistic children strategies that help them to survive in world made for neurotypicals?

Juliet was somewhat of a pioneer when it came to standing her ground in the schoolyard. The teacher's comments about Gabriel having a problem were not only confronting, they were unhelpful. So when the school didn't deliver, she innovated. "The school couldn't give me any leads," she explains. "Well what do I do now, I thought? Where do I go? It was like, he's got a problem, we don't know what it is, we'll just leave that with you and you go and find someone to identify it. Bye, see you later, with no support and definitely no emotional support."

Juliet did what she had done in the past and turned to her passion for gardening. She'd always used gardens for relaxation and sensed that they could be a respite tool for Gabriel and other children. With spade, pitchfork and, thankfully, the school's backing, she began work on transforming the gardens around the school into a living chill-out zone.

"The teachers had observed that Gabriel was spending all of his lunchtimes and recess running from one playground to another, and the school had quite a few playgrounds," says Juliet. "He was totally disoriented and that was creating quite a bit of anxiety. And you can't learn when you're in that state.

"I met a mother who was part of an environment group and it was her invitation to get involved that actually helped me to make the first step toward finding any sort of solution to Gabriel's needs. If you can get hold of the anxiety, you can move forward, and I found I could treat the anxiety in the garden."

With the help of other parents and children, Juliet planted flowers and vegetables and paved pathways throughout the green space. She brought in chairs, so children could sit amid nature, away from the noise and activity of the schoolyard. She created artworks in the form of mosaics, and signs about the plants so children could learn more about botany and the environment. She organised a tree-planting day. And a buddy system where younger children were paired with an older child on a garden project—a programme that still exists in the school today.

"When Gabriel interacted with his buddy, it was the first time he actually understood why you would want to relate to other children," says Juliet.

Juliet didn't realise it at the time, but through art and gardening she was developing a therapeutic environment that had a flow-on effect for Gabriel's learning in the classroom, and no doubt for other children's learning too.

"The connection to peace and tranquility, I wanted that for Gabriel. The connection to tactile experiences like clay or earth, I wanted for Gabriel. Having worked as an art teacher, I knew how art helped small children make the transition into a different learning environment—going from play to less play, sitting and paying attention and not touching and not wriggling. Like art, gardens do provide that different setting for learning and a place to just be. And, as I later found out, art and gardens are spot-on for kids on the spectrum."

Children, both neurotypical and those with ASD, are believed to be happier, smarter and better adjusted with more time spent outdoors. Nature is linked to restorative benefits, and sharper focus. For children with sensory issues, a garden can be a place of peace and quiet, order and calm.[32] Many school playgrounds now incorporate tactile features such as a sandbox, a pebble path or water. Much of this is thanks to parent volunteers such as Juliet. She went on to set up gardens, places of tranquility, at several schools in Melbourne, including Gabriel's high school, a public school with a class for children with autism. Subsequently, Juliet has received awards for her gardening efforts—recognition that such labours have helped countless children, whether on the spectrum or not.

I am overawed at Juliet's generosity and dedication to her son, not to mention to other children. But I am very aware that all of this has been volunteer work and I can't help but wonder how she affords to spend so much time out of paid work. Like many parents, I have volunteered to help with various activities at school, but in recent years I've had to pull back as the necessity of paid work to meet a mortgage and the cost of raising two children, takes over. Juliet also looks after her elderly mother for much of the week, leaving little if any time for paid work. I feel rude asking but, ignoring my inner etiquette, I blurt out: "Are you making an income at all? How do you afford to do it?"

"Thank you for asking," she surprisingly responds. "It's not until people bother to ask that they actually realise that I did have a career. I was in publishing and advertising, which didn't gel with the lifestyle of being a single mum and having a child with a disability. It doesn't matter what the severity of the disability, you still have to deal with ethical issues, with issues of energy and the sheer reality of fitting everything in.

"You have to find work that can fit into flexible hours—work that will allow you to take your child to therapy in the middle of the day. Even if you do hold down a full-time job and your child is the type of kid who can handle afterschool care, if there is any afterschool care available, you can't take them to appointments after 5pm so you have to finish work early. There's another juggle to think about."

Steve Silberman discovered while researching *Neurotribes* that: "it was not unusual for parents whose finances were already strained by the cost of behavioural interventions to have to walk away from careers they loved to effectively become case managers for their children."[33] In 2013 the National Disability Insurance Scheme Act was passed in Australia to help families afford the cost of support. While this has helped very many people, others have found it to be slow and cumbersome. At the time of writing, I, for one, am still waiting for an outcome on to the application I lodged seven months ago.

The early days of Tom's therapy were incredibly expensive. There were paediatrician appointments, psychology, occupational therapy and an array of other therapies we dabbled in, such as the chiropractor or the expensive computer brain-training programme, the bills for which my father paid. Who knows what helped and what didn't? Perhaps it wasn't all necessary but, wherever we turned, 'early intervention' was the catch-cry. Looking back, I think we were fearful of the consequences if we didn't try a therapy, particularly one that a trusted source may have suggested. Perhaps 'this' was the solution, or if not that then 'this'. Inevitably we would start to see results of a new therapy for the first few weeks, until Tom and I grew tired of juggling the appointments or the money dried up. These days we have pulled right back and our focus is on learning support in the way of tutoring. But still there is no way we could have afforded any of it if I wasn't working. I chose to leave permanent employment and instead work flexible hours, partly because James's job as a freelancer had no routine or predictability. But I took what writing work I could get in order to make ends meet—writing for magazines about everything from babies and parenting to scientific research.

"But how do you support yourself?" I blurt out again to Juliet, taken aback by my own brazenness. I hate asking questions about money. I think it's something my parents instilled in me. Never ask a person's age or what income they earn. Yet I'm fascinated. How does she do it?

"Well, I'm lucky that I always had some money in the bank. But you also change your lifestyle. You start saying, we can't have a holiday, or no, we can't have a TV, or no, I don't do whatever I like doing in my spare time. And I've met along the way many, many families, and most of them are women on their own, and that is something that really is a pressing issue. Financial pressures are huge for families with children on the spectrum."

Juliet has obviously been very careful with her money and made some serious sacrifices. She's been far more careful than James and I. If we want something we tend to find a way, and that way inevitably involves working our butts off. As stressful as our financial situation can sometimes feel, having two freelancers in the family, we have never gone without. Our children have everything they need and more, and we have been fortunate enough to have some wonderful memories of family holidays—which admittedly I have had to fight for, but also made possible through my various work projects. I'm currently saving for a family holiday to Europe, which feels awfully ambitious, and indulgent in light of the conversation I've just had with Juliet.

Of course there is no right or wrong way. Everyone does it differently. We're all just stumbling through the fog trying to make sense of our situations. Trying to make ends meet. Trying to ensure our children are happy and supported. Trying to ensure that we as parents are happy too.

"I think one of the biggest things is that a strong parent will find a way," Juliet offers. "You can have a lot of different support networks, which helps. But unless you are strong within yourself, unless you can see the path clearly, or even slightly clearly, then it's not going to happen. You can't rely on schools for direction, or on therapy for that matter. First you have to get yourself in a better place.

"That might mean making adjustments. It might mean finding another career. It might mean totally reducing your budget. But then, it also might mean seeking support from friends, or parents, or services where you can connect and perhaps start creating a broader network. It's hard to ask for help. Many people can't actually go to someone they don't know. But if it means getting yourself in a better place, then you have to do it. You have to do it for you, and for your child."

She's right. A friend traversing some rocky terrain with a teenage daughter recently sent me this quote, which I have printed out and placed prominently above my desk:

"A lighthouse is a clear, predictable and consistent guide standing firmly on safe ground to guide one to safety. When the seas are roughest a lighthouse stands firm. The lighthouse doesn't wade into the water to rescue, but provides stability and hope to those struggling to make the shore."[34]

It's hard to be a predictable, guiding force, particularly when there are rough seas. What is the key? Persistence? Self-confidence? At the table from which I write this, in a café near my home, I have observed a number of mothers with their children. The bubbly and relaxed mother, laughing and speaking to her two boys like they are her greatest mates. The tired, cranky mother of three, reminding her well-behaved little girls to use their manners and drink their hot chocolate neatly. The mother and son who hardly speak, yet both happily read their books and share a croissant. The Italian mother spending valuable time with a friend, while her baby falls asleep eating spaghetti. Each scenario is so delightful it its own way. Each mother and each child is so different to the next. Each one of them is navigating their own life stories and seeing what the day brings.

Through the looking glass

Catherine & Louis

It is a Saturday, so there are no children at the preschool today. But there are plenty of signs of life—rudimentary paintings strung up with pegs on a makeshift clothesline, hardened Play-Doh stuck to the table, misplaced hats and random tricycles scattered along the meandering garden path. We are sitting at a children's table, our bottoms squeezed onto miniature chairs. And this is all happening on an island in the middle of the Pacific Ocean. I cannot disclose exactly which island because of privacy, but let's just say that we're a long way from nowhere.

I feel like Alice down the rabbit hole, my long legs bent up like a wishbone. Sitting opposite me is not the White Rabbit, but Catherine, teacher and director of the preschool. In her spare time she is an artist, an actor and a mother of three.

"I'm not the tidiest of teachers," admits Catherine. "But we have a lot of fun."

I spy a trampoline through the trees. "You have a trampoline? In a preschool?" I ask. Having once worked at a magazine about early childhood education, I am well aware of the restrictions placed on preschools because of liability issues. A trampoline would never be allowed in Sydney.

"Like I said, we have a lot of fun," she smiles.

I believe it. Catherine oozes a positivity that the cynic in me finds positively curious. Her enthusiasm isn't contrived or pollyannaish. She is simply very energetic and optimistic. Of course, it could have something to do with the idyllic existence she leads on a tropical island—a paradise of rainforests, picture-perfect beaches and rolling green hills dotted with sheep. As we converse, I can feel the layers of a frenetic city existence peel away and the serenity of island life start to rub off. A mobile chimes in the depths of the garden. A cool, gentle ocean breeze rustles the palm fronds above, shooting darts of sunlight through a canopy filter. When I lick my lips I taste sea salt.

"It's a beautiful place that's for sure. But the best thing about this place is that it's so safe for kids," muses Catherine. "The community spirit here is amazing."

It is true that the island has an old-fashioned country feel about it. Drivers wave to each other and to pedestrians as they pass by on the road. Apparently nobody locks their doors. When I check into my apartment, I discover the back door doesn't even have a lock. Children walk around barefoot and free, their parents safe in the knowledge that community spirit looms large, and even if they don't know where their child is, somebody will. While I think I might go stir-crazy being this far from any other civilisation, Catherine says it is a wonderful place to raise a family.

Catherine's eldest of three children is 12 year old Louis. A striking-looking young man with an olive complexion and jet-black hair, Louis maintains eye contact when he speaks. He appears engaged and genuinely interested, asking questions about Sydney and telling me about his school camps to Uluru and Canberra. Such conversation is quite remarkable for any boy fast approaching adolescence. I certainly would never guess he was on the autism spectrum. Louis doesn't stay and chat to me for long, as he is due at the local café, where he volunteers his time to make sandwiches and wash dishes. He says he'd like to get a paid job there when he's 14, the age he's legally allowed to work. But for now he's happy picking up new skills and chatting to the chef and customers. He bids me farewell with "have a lovely day" and I think, what a charming boy. He seems to have everything going for him.

Catherine first picked up on Louis' autism when he was a 10-month-old baby. This is particularly young, as many of the indicators of autism are not evident until children start socialising in an early childhood education setting around the age three or beyond. But Catherine's nine-year-old nephew had recently been diagnosed with Asperger's and this was top of mind when Louis was a baby. She was also trained as a preschool teacher and had been around babies and toddlers for several years, and so knew what was developmentally typical.

"When Louis was about eight or nine months old we were in a mother's group and I noticed that his social behavior was completely different to that of the other babies," explains Catherine. "He wasn't interested in the other children and would just gravitate towards the adults all of the time. His eye contact was different, he didn't smile as much as the other kids and he was just socially very different to the other kids that were developing at that same age.

"I was so lucky that my brother and sister-in-law did all the hard work for me by getting the diagnosis for my nephew. I was immensely grateful to them. They went through nine long years of not knowing why their child was different or ostracised at school.

When they rang us to tell us of my nephew's diagnosis, I jumped on Google and went tick, tick, tick. Here I was with a 10-month-old baby thinking 'ding!'—light bulb moment."

At the time, Catherine and her husband John were living on the mainland. They both loved acting and were involved in amateur theatre. They both worked in secure jobs and had ready access to medical professionals. Catherine's suspicions about her baby were later confirmed by a paediatrician, who officially diagnosed Louis with Asperger's. And that's when Catherine assumed her role as Louis' advocate. She knew that there was little knowledge about autism in her community, and the wider society, and determined that she would have to change that to ensure her son would not be misunderstood. She made the decision to always be honest and up-front about his autism—with Louis and with others.

"I have always been very open about Louis' Asperger's. I guess I just thought we were better off telling people what it was and how they could help, rather than saying he's just different, or trying to gloss over it. People still say to me that I opened their eyes so much more as to how to deal with other people and be more mindful of all of the different personalities in the world."

Louis too has never hidden his autism. Catherine has instead encouraged him to be brave and up-front if he's confused about a social cue or doesn't understand something by saying: "I have Asperger's and that's part of the reason I don't understand. Could you please explain it to me another way?"

She has taught him that there is no need to feel any shame around his autism. Rather, it is just a part of who he is. Catherine also knew that she needed to educate people, teachers included, about how best to understand her boy.

"We knew that his social skills weren't the best, that he spoke like an adult at the age of four, and so it was pretty obvious that people were having some difficulty knowing how best to approach this. Better to bring it up with them than everyone just try and ignore the obvious."

It hasn't always been easy though. Children can be insensitive and Louis' differences did not go unnoticed in some social circles. Many six-year-olds would prefer to kick a ball than talk about tectonic plates or the topography of Pompeii, for example. But generally, Catherine's open approach has held Louis in good stead. The small community on the island knows Louis, and Catherine feels that this nurturing environment will help give him the confidence to move forward into adulthood later on. Louis was three years old when they moved to the island from the mainland, and the decision to do so was very much around his wellbeing. Not only did Catherine and John want to bring their children up in a safe and idyllic environment, but they recognised the benefits of having one school where primary and high school were all under the same roof. They relished the idea of Louis having the same class of children from kindergarten to Year 12, and they, the same families. It is a risk in some ways (what happens if you get stuck with a class of ratbags for 12 years, and on an island no less?) and a set-up that wouldn't suit everyone, but it has certainly paid off for this family.

At the age of 12, Louis has already chosen the university in Sydney that he wants to attend once he leaves school. A brainiac with an encyclopedic knowledge of all things 'natural disasters', he plans to study volcanology. Louis started reading at an early age, with Catherine's help and encouragement, and was reading encyclopedias by the age of five. Catherine describes it as an interest that came naturally to him. It was never forced upon him, rather he actively sought information to sate his voracious appetite.

"He could talk about natural disasters until the cows come home," is how Catherine puts it. "He started borrowing books on volcanoes from the school library when he was in kindergarten. The librarian said if you're sick of them, we'll put a stop to it. But I said go for it. If he's interested in it let him read everything about it.

"Around that time, a university student came over to the island on holidays. She was studying volcanology and we sort of befriended her, through Louis, our budding volcanologist. She went away and came back again eight months later and was testing Louis on all things volcanoes, asking him really long words and stuff I'd never even heard of. Here was our five-year-old having a conversation about pyroclastic flow and all of these sorts of amazing things. She said that in eight months, he had learnt more from books than she had learnt at uni. She said 'we haven't started learning about that stuff in the third year of uni and he's got it sussed already'."

I notice a swelling pride when Catherine speaks to me about Louis. Not in a boastful way, just in a way that's supportive of the interests he has chosen to pursue. The latest addition to Louis's list of fascinating research topics is air crash investigations, the more dramatic the better, as he Googles and YouTubes and reads until he can no more. She describes how he has written, directed and filmed short films about air crashes for a school project. Not surprisingly, the project received very high marks and even cemented some temporary friendships. But while natural disasters and air crashes excite Louis and can spawn hours of adult conversation, children are only prepared to listen to so much. When I ask Catherine if Louis currently has any close friends she says "no, not really" and behind her radiant positivity, I detect the first hint of sadness.

"I think it was hardest when he was probably four or five and he'd walk into a social situation and everyone would roll their eyes and go 'here comes Louis'. He was oblivious, I think, but it would break my heart. Absolutely break my heart.

"These days he gets sad. At times he really wants friends, but it's so difficult for him. He gets on better with girls than boys, possibly because he has six girl cousins and he understands them better. But of course now as the teenage years set in, there are no more sleepovers or play dates with the girls from school. He can't understand how the boys around town just want to wear their caps backwards and hang out at the skate ramp all day—and that's every boy in his class. There's nothing interesting, fun or educational about that for him. He doesn't get boys the same age and they don't get him. He will probably never really fit in until he's in uni and he's with like-minded people."

Children on the autism spectrum have a notoriously difficult time making friends. For a start, reading social cues, facial expressions and body language do not come intuitively. I imagine it would be like something akin to trying to get by in a foreign culture where you know little of the language or mannerisms. Barry M. Prizant writes:

Nearly every person with autism has some degree of difficulty navigating the social world. Some…are so oblivious to social convention that they aren't aware of their own blunders and pay little attention to how others perceive their actions. Others…struggle in a different way: they are all too cognisant that social rules and expectations exist, but since they don't intuitively understand them, they often feel anxious and their self-esteem suffers as they struggle to negotiate a world that seems to defy their grasp.[35]

I remember when we visited Cambodia as a family and we were surprised to find the locals would enthusiastically pinch Otis's cheek wherever we went. Only five at the time, the poor little thing was often left stunned, red-cheeked and tearful until some friends explained that it was because they thought him so cute. After that he took it as a compliment and laughed. But for a while he thought they were trying to hurt him because he didn't comprehend that particular social convention. For people on the autism spectrum, neurotypes are an equally as baffling bunch, and negotiating how to socialise can be like walking on a tight rope—a balancing act between naïveté and paranoia. To the person with autism, neurotypes often speak in riddles. Sometimes, those jokes are meant to be funny, but sometimes they are mean. Even tone of voice can be an enigma. Take a laugh or a smile, for example, which can mean so many things, not all of them good. In my role as a university tutor, many of my students are from diverse cultural backgrounds and I need to explicitly explain irony, sarcasm and many of the clichés and idioms that Australians take for granted. Even the students born in Australia often need direction because their parents do not speak English or are not familiar with our colloquialisms. Negotiating the playground for a child on the spectrum is perhaps a little like speaking English as a second language.

Added to the confusion of verbal and body language is a lack of spatial awareness in some children. Tom always keeps a physical distance from people, never quite knowing how close to stand. Lately, I've also noticed that he has lacks awareness of the people around him, even if they are an arm's distance away. I will say to him "who was that boy standing next to you" and he'll have no idea that there was anyone there. Other challenges, such as inattention or auditory processing difficulties, sensory overload and social anxiety can all wreak havoc when it comes to social interactions in the playground—not to mention bullies, the schoolyard pecking order and the general confusion of adolescence. Teasing and bullying can be long-lasting, affecting a person's self-esteem and contributing to their social anxiety. The literature unfortunately states that bullying is inevitable for a child on the spectrum.[36] Attwood cites a study of the prevalence and frequency of bullying in a sample of more than 400 children with Asperger's aged between four and 17.[37] It found the "reported rate of bullying to be at least four times higher than for their [neurotypical] peers. More than 90 per cent of mothers of children with Asperger's syndrome who completed the survey reported that their children had been the target of some form of bullying within the previous year."

Such realities are never too far away, but I get the impression that Catherine doesn't like to dwell on the negatives, not from what I can see anyway. I'm sure this contributes to Louis' outlook. He certainly strikes me as being fairly resilient and socially adept, more so than many neurotypical children of his age. And I'm sure that much of this points back to Catherine's approach toward Louis, where she has encouraged him to confidently tell people who he is and why he might experience the world a little differently. Rather than instill a sense of shame about his difference, she has embraced it. Rather than be fearful of how he might fit in, she has celebrated his uniqueness and subsequently he feels comfortable in his own skin.

Barry M. Prizant, author of *Uniquely Human*, believes that how we respond to our children can affect their feelings about themselves. Parents, for example, might want to curb their children's behaviour so that the child might be more socially accepted, but this might send a message of shame. He states:

> It's totally understandable that a parent may want their child not to engage in behaviours that look different or that are attention-getting in public or that may be stigmatising for a child. But the bottom line is; what are we communicating to a child if we're always saying stop that, don't do that, always correcting? There's a lot of attention now being paid to the impact of what we do on a child and eventually an adult's self-esteem.[38]

I ponder how Tom prefers to fly under the radar at school. He's not one to openly discuss his autism or do anything that might draw attention to it or to himself. But this is in part personality, rather than learned behaviour. He has a quiet personality, and likes to be an observer rather than the centre of attention. Meanwhile, I consider the 'learned behavior' aspect of his approach quite clever and insightful, and it takes the edge off his everyday social challenges. As much as I would like him to feel comfortable enough to wholeheartedly be himself, I also admire his ability to use discretion—and to choose the right moment to show off his differences in all of their richness and colour. It is a common paradox. We want our kids to be self-assured enough to let down their guard, but we don't want them to get hurt.

Certain facial expressions, such as smiling in response to another's smile, eye contact, the ability to make small talk, to laugh at yourself—all of these are learned social skills for many people on the spectrum. And Louis has mastered all of them. Having outgoing and theatrical parents would help, with Catherine and John both working in community theatre. Louis's younger siblings also love to perform. His sister sings and plays guitar, and his little brother enjoys dress-ups whenever given the chance.

"Our first production after Louis was born was *Chicago*," says Catherine. "John was the lead and I was one of the girls. Louis slept in a portacot in the theatre and practically took his first steps on stage."

But while Louis may be good at thrusting himself onto centrestage, literally and metaphorically, Catherine is always in the wings, gently nudging him into the spotlight. "I do feel that I have pushed him," she says. "I push him beyond his comfort barriers with every situation we go in to, just that little bit further than he wants to go. I know there are times when it's uncomfortable for him but I stretch him and hope that the next time it's not quite so hard. Sometimes of course he'll just throw his hands up and go and lock himself in a room or just sit in the car all night. That's all part of it too. There are times when I can see the depression falling in, but then I come up with some great idea, like let's make movies. It's a matter of always being on top of it and trying to find a way that can be helpful."

I too feel like a stagehand in the wings most days, coaxing my reluctant actor to try new and different roles. Trying to catch him when he falls. Letting him fall lightly enough so he's not hurt, but letting him fall all the same so he learns how to land by himself next time. But this role of stagehand is one that is exhausting. It's relentless and thankless and selfless. How does Catherine keep going? Does she never feel resentful? If she does, she doesn't show it. Nor does she let on if she's resentful about doing the vast majority of parenting.

"John and I have sort of fallen into these very traditional roles," she explains. "He does it his way, I do it my way and we catch up somewhere in the middle. He goes to work, I look after the kids, even though I'm working too of course, but the preschool is sort of like my extended family home. My kids come here after school. It's another place they can feel safe."

As well as working through the day, John works three or four evenings a week.

"It's really not a problem. John and I were married for 12 years before we had Louis and I knew what

I was getting myself into when I had him. I would see these parents come and pick their kids up from preschool and I knew they were tired. I knew it was going to be hard work. And I had no expectations that John was going to be home every night helping me cook dinner. We didn't have a normal home life with all the theatre. I didn't expect routine to suddenly appear out of thin air."

I listen non-judgmentally. I listen wholeheartedly. And then I reflect and think how differently I feel about being the primary carer. I did that for a number of years and it drove me mad. Brought up by a staunchly feminist mother, I detest the thought of falling into the traditional role of homemaker. I fight it with every bone in my body, and I find it boring. Cleaning, cooking, childcare should all be shared roles. But of course in reality they're not and that upsets me. Catherine sees things differently. She doesn't feel exploited or undermined. She says she has chosen to fulfill the role of primary carer because of the proximity it gives her to Louis and her other children. She understands Louis, she 'gets him', and that means she is the best person for the job. I just wonder how many mothers are in the same boat. How many mothers are carrying the responsibility of care, education and advocacy? I'm sure there are many mothers who feel they are the best person to do so, but do they really have a choice?

"I think it's hard for John because he doesn't get it, and I suppose I threw myself into it all when Louis was little," explains Catherine. "I was doing all the research and just feeding it back to John. He didn't have the same level of interest."

Catherine says the other reason she 'gets it' is because the autism link comes from her side of the family. As well as her diagnosed nephew, she believes her brother and father could in fact be 'Aspies'. She even thinks she may have been diagnosed if she were a child today. An artistic girl, she had great trouble forming relationships with other children at school.

"But you're so chatty and sociable," I laugh.

"It manifests in different ways," says Catherine. "My nephew and brother are introverted instrument technicians. They can pull things apart, rebuild a car in a weekend but they don't enjoy social situations. My dad and I, on the other hand, are probably more like Louis. We can talk under water. My dad was a chief steward with an airline and would recite the same monologue every single trip. He would even recite it to us kids and we'd heard it a million times, but we just accepted it. When the younger boys were diagnosed, we just thought aha! Now it makes so much more sense—that repetition of a story and having to start right at the very beginning and keep going until it's finished."

Catherine's innate understanding of autism is certainly complemented by her work as an early childhood educator, but she has thrown herself into researching the subject with gusto. Without the luxury of a therapist on the island, she has had to rely on her intuition. A paediatrician visits the island every so often, but this is only a recent development and was not available to Louis when he was little and in need of early intervention. That intervention and support has come in the form of Catherine. As well as primary carer, she is researcher, counsel, advocate, educator and provider of emotional support. She is also a mentor to other families on the island who have children on the spectrum, families who might be going through the initial confusion that comes with a new diagnosis. From a place of her own confusion and uncertainty, Catherine's role has grown into one of wisdom and guidance.

I am reminded of an article our paediatrician gave us about children like Louis and Tom, who are genetically predisposed to vulnerability, but who are raised in safe and secure environments. In *The Atlantic*, David Dobbs theorises that there are two types of people: dandelions, which can take root and thrive anywhere; and orchids, which are "fragile and fickle, but capable of blooming spectacularly if given greenhouse care".[39] Drawing on genealogy, psychology and scientific experiments with Rhesus monkeys,

Dobbs concludes that 'orchid' genes have an evolutionary role in humanity. While prone to depression, anxiety, antisocial or self-destructive behavior, vulnerable children can in fact give back to society in vast and surprising ways when nurtured. He writes: "With a bad environment and poor parenting, orchid children can end up depressed, drug-addicted or in jail—but with the right environment and good parenting, they can grow up to be society's most creative, successful, and happy people." Such findings are strangely encouraging. There is a lot of pressure for a parent to provide the perfect greenhouse conditions, but Dobbs' words do buoy me. "Risk becomes possibility; vulnerability becomes plasticity and responsiveness," he writes. He goes on to cite paediatrician W. Thomas Boyce who says the orchid hypothesis "profoundly recasts the way we think about human frailty...We see that when kids with this kind of vulnerability are put in the right setting, they don't merely do better than before, they do the best—even better, that is, than their peers." It offers pause for thought and the motivation to carry on.

But the orchid hypothesis also worries me. What about the other vulnerable children who fall through the gaps? Those whose parents aren't as positive or resilient or educated or clued up as the Catherines of the world. The ones whose parents who may not speak English, or can't afford to seek professional advice?

What about the orchids who are exposed to pests or drought, despite their parents' good intentions? Those who are exposed to bullying, for example, or are neglected by an under-resourced school system?

In her essay *Teaching Australia* in the *Griffith Review*, author and former teacher GJ Stroud writes about being morally conflicted by not being able to assist the vulnerable children in her kindergarten class. These are children who struggle with learning difficulties, or who come to school having no breakfast in their belly and no sandwich in their lunchbox. She writes about the changing face of teaching and the pressure placed on students to perform in assessments, not to mention the pressure on teachers to keep up with bureaucratic standards. Such complex issues keep Stroud awake at night and ultimately result in her having a breakdown and retiring from teaching.

"Schools should not be framed by business models," she writes. "They should not be viewed in terms of academic results based on productivity. When we look at schools in this way we lose sight of what matters. We lose sight of students."[40]

Many of those students are so-called 'orchid' children. Despite the tenacity of their parents, they can still be let down by a system that doesn't have the time or space for them. And I suppose that's when we as a society need to question what we can do to embrace those orchid children, rather than just tolerate them. Schools need to make space for everyone, to embrace diversity, to teach children about bullying and responsible relationships, but adults need to get on board too. We not only have a responsibility as parents to look after our own children, but other people's children as well.

Louis is fortunate. He not only has the support of his parents and his teachers, but also his community, who, thanks to Catherine, appreciate his challenges and his strengths. When Catherine decided to support the international autism awareness campaign 'Light it Blue' a few years back, she didn't just stick up a Facebook post. She managed to get an entire island's community behind the idea and turn it into a fundraising event. The local café made cupcakes with blue icing to sell, and the townsfolk bought up big on blue light globes to light up old heritage buildings along the foreshore. In the evening, they all gathered on the beach to commune and celebrate. Surrounded by his people, Louis gave a moving speech:

Hi, my name is Louis. I'm eight years old and have Asperger's syndrome. I don't like people using loud voices, it makes me feel like I am in a battle zone. Lots of people and kids don't understand Asperger's. All I would like is for people to understand and accept that we are all different but we have some amazing qualities and skills to share with the world. So please try and speak calmly as we have feelings too.

Lots of people with Asperger's have made a difference in the world like Einstein and Thomas Edison. I want to be a famous architect and make a difference in this world too by redesigning places like Christchurch earthquake zone and the Brisbane flood area, Japan's tsunami area and W.A. bushfire region. I want to make a difference and make the world a better place.

Of course, he's already making the world a better place. And so is his mum.

As our conversation winds up, I hoist myself up off my miniature seat and survey the lush, tropical garden that envelops the preschool and stretches beyond, across the island. I reach out and touch green, downy moss crawling up a palm tree. I breathe in the briny sea air. And I ponder, what a perfect Wonderland for a rare and resplendent flower.

Mushrooms and marjoram

Alex & Sylvia

When Alex was a boy he refused to sit at the family table for meals. The overpowering smell of home cooking, often with garlic and onions and other produce from the family farm, was too much for him to bear, so he would sit in the living room eating a separately prepared, bland meal. His Sicilian paternal grandmother Maria was mortified that her grandson would not join the family at mealtime, let alone eat the traditional staple of pasta, and one day chased Alex into the kitchen with a stick. His mother Sylvia went to her bedroom and cried.

Nevertheless, Sylvia continued to buy Alex prepackaged food from the supermarket. She was not immune to the stares of onlookers as she loaded her trolley full of frozen pizza, nuggets, chips and pies. But it was easier than having to deal with the meltdowns at home—meltdowns that might last an hour and which baffled Sylvia and left her feeling emotionally and physically exhausted. Little did she know that her son would one day excel in cooking and his unique sense of smell would hold him in good stead, advising customers on herbs and flavours and devising complex recipes. At age 22, Alex is an integral member of his family's fresh produce business, mainly known for its tomato varieties of hearty rich heirlooms, cherry and grape tomatoes. Alex's paternal grandfather Alfonso started growing tomatoes more than 50 years ago. He died two years before Alex was born, but the legacy continues with the family's farm on the outskirts of Sydney, now managed by Carlo, Alex's father. The farm sits atop a hill and looks out across other market farms in the area. A small and humble farmhouse is dwarfed by a large work shed, which houses tractors and crates of vegetables ready for sale. On the horizon, in the far off distance, are skyscrapers.

On weekends, the family heads toward those monolithic buildings to manage a stall at a busy growers market, a haunt for inner-city hipster foodies. There, the family sells tomatoes, as well as cucumbers, capsicums, eggplants, beans, chilli and aromatic herbs. When I visit the market, Alex and his family are run off their feet, with customers filling their baskets with produce from the colourful stall of reds and greens and yellows. It startles me that one farm can spawn so much colour. As I approach I notice that Alex is engaged in conversation with one of the customers. He is holding a bunch of marjoram in one hand. "You can't have mushrooms without marjoram. They are natural bedfellows," I hear him enthuse.

Sylvia spies me, smiles and endearingly rolls her eyes. In an earlier conversation she spoke of Alex's innate sense of matching flavours—of identifying subtle differences in ingredients and pairing strong or delicate flavours together in surprising ways.

"He seems to have a natural ability with herbs and he can associate flavours of food," says Sylvia. "I overheard him at the markets giving an old lady the recipe for broad bean soup. He's never even cooked broad bean soup. It was just instinctive. She came back a week later, said she'd tried it and it was fantastic."

Like Sylvia, Alex's dad Carlo speaks with a sense of pride about his son. "It was a bit 'doom and gloom' when he was younger, but he's just evolved into a wonderful human being," he muses. "It was hard in the early years, especially for Sylvia, because she was with him during the day while I was on the farm. But he has really taught us, me especially, to be a lot more of a patient person as a consequence.

"There were times when he would push my buttons, or he would chew my ear off about his special interest of the time, whether that be spiders or Pokémon or star signs, or whatever, and I thought, I don't know, this is really not my cup of tea. But then I'd learn something I didn't know. He would talk about history for example and recall unusual things that happened at that time in history—stuff you wouldn't normally learn, like the colour of someone's shirt or their favourite food. He can be a good teacher, if you give him your time. I create time if he wants it."

Carlo reflects how a manager echoed these sentiments of 'Alex as mentor' when Alex did work experience at a local country club.

"One night when we picked him up the boss said 'Alex has actually taught us about cooking. We used to just garnish our food with parsley. He knows a lot more than I do about which herbs go with what dishes' and he wrote the most glowing reference. It was all true. He used to cook us dinner and he'd cook fish or steak and the way he used herbs or make his own version of tomato salad was just unbelievable."

These days, Alex is Carlo's sidekick. They help each other out immensely and the family is proud of what the business has become. They were thrilled to recently discover that Alex had organised matching t-shirts for the family to wear at the markets. He designed them, ordered them and paid for them without any consultation or assistance.

Throughout the week, Alex works as a barista at a café in the city. While his dream of working as a chef has been shelved for now, following a stressful six-month stint in a commercial kitchen, he is writing a cookbook and plans to open a restaurant with his best friend sometime in the future. Although Alex lives alone in a rented apartment these days, Sylvia says he still offers his mum tips in the kitchen when he visits for dinner. "It can be annoying when he says 'Mum you're making meatballs do you have sage in there? Oh you're cooking chicken, did you put lemon thyme in that one?' It's frustrating when I'm just trying to put food on the table but I laugh it off, especially when you consider he was a kid who once hated food, who would dry retch if you made him sit at the table or throw a wobbly if we went to a restaurant. To think that tomato salad with basil would send him off. Now he's offering advice on how best to serve it!"

I feel guilty taking Alex away from the busy market stall but Sylvia and Carlo assure me they'll manage while I chat to him. Alex is 22 now—a polite and quietly spoken man, his gentleness juxtaposed against his tall and strong-looking frame. As we walk away, his maternal grandmother Jean, also working on the market stall, taps me on the shoulder and offers:

"He's growing up into a fine young man, so sweet and hardworking. He'll go far." It's hard to imagine this gentle giant ever having meltdowns, throwing his body around and hitting his mum. Apparently he used to call Jean the "nanna from hell" and lock her out of the house. But he says it wasn't personal: "I used to lock everyone out, or inside the house, just to get away from them." Such outbursts have obviously not tainted his relationships within the family. In fact, from what I can tell, the family is particularly close. The first thing Alex says to me when I start my tape recorder rolling is: "I want to thank my family because they've always been so supportive of me. I couldn't be where I am now without them."

Alex can't remember when he actually found out he had Asperger's, but Sylvia tells me he was diagnosed at six years old, at a time when a lot less was known about the condition. When I ask Alex how autism has affected his life, he shrugs. "It's who I am. I don't know any different." And I realise what a silly question that is. Of course it is simply a part of who he is, and I feel rude almost, for asking it.

"I like to look at the positives," he continues. "There's a little saying I have and that is, 'In life we must accept ourselves for who and what we are. That is the road to happiness'. The key is knowing who you are. Life is all about discovering yourself. That took me years to find out of course. It's been a hard journey but I have found that almost every year I am a different, evolving person and everything that I've gone through has made me the person I am today."

It strikes me that Alex has experienced a lot in his 22 years, but it is through these difficulties that he has developed such a philosophical outlook. I was not expecting Alex to be quite so forthcoming, or proffer such wisdom so quickly. Unlike many men in Australian society, Alex is comfortable speaking about his emotions. Despite a somewhat rocky start to life, Alex certainly seems to be very comfortable in his own skin now. "I believe I'm my own person. It's who I am and I can't change it. I mean I've become a man with many talents. When I'm working as a barista, I can remember at least 180 people's coffee orders. I see their face and I know what they want...large cappuccino, one sugar; small skim latte, extra hot; long black, one sugar..."

He also boasts an uncanny ability to 'visualise' flavours without actually smelling or tasting them. "I can visually memorise a flavour and match that flavour to a herb or to another flavour. I can sort of guess which flavours complement each other and of course trial and error helps as well."

As well visualising the flavours, he also, ironically, uses his hypersensitive sense of smell to inform his ingredient choices. Where once the smell of flavours was too much to bear, it now helps him creates exquisite dishes—mostly with an Italian, French or Spanish influence. Over time, his sense of taste has changed dramatically.

"As a kid I was a very fussy eater, but over the years my tastebuds kicked in," he explains. "So many things didn't appeal to me as a kid because the smell and taste was too rich, too powerful. Eggplant for example. As a kid I used to hate it and now as an adult I love it. It's one of my favourite vegetables to eat and to prepare."

Alex's understanding of herbs and flavours is supplemented by his experience of growing them on the farm, and now in the garden of his small city apartment. At one stage, he was growing 16 different types of mint: "Some of the ones I really like are apple mint, American peppermint, lemon mint, chocolate mint, even ginger mint or Egyptian mint." I personally had no idea mint was so diverse.

He tells me of a favourite recipe, partly inspired by the same Sicilian grandmother Maria who chased him with a stick. She lived with the family after Alfonso died and despite being a strict disciplinarian she would whisper to Alex that he was her 'favourite'. Thankfully, when Alex hit puberty his penchant for frozen food began to wane and he started eating pasta. He and Maria soon bonded over cooking. Alex recalls his grandmother's cooking with great fondness. "She was really a very good cook. The only thing I used to dislike was something called *due uova*, Italian for two eggs. Whenever she cooked them she used a handful of salt and I hated it. It was just too salty for my taste." Not surprisingly, Alex was devastated when she passed away, but he still thinks of her when he cooks. "So my favourite recipe goes like this. Basically the sauce is olive oil, garlic, a little bit of brandy, hot chilli, chorizo and it's all just mixed through. I like it with lots of hot, hot chilli. Sometimes I'll even add just a dash of white wine to give it a little bit of sweetness." It's a recipe that sounds like it packs plenty of punch, especially for someone who would only eat very plain food once upon a time.

"There are now only three things in the world that I don't eat. Number one is tuna, number two is cucumber and number three is anchovies. They're too salty. My dad eats them out of the tin. Urggh! I like sweet, sour, spicy, bitter, but salty, no, that's not a flavour I've adapted to. The cucumber is just because we grew so many on the farm and I got sick of picking them and sick of the sight of them, so I'm not much fussed about their taste."

Other than cucumbers, Alex's memories of growing up on a farm are fond, particularly because of the space and freedom that it allowed. "My earliest memory, a memory I've always kept close to my heart is me at four years old. We had stone fruit, acres and acres of stone fruit, peaches, plums, nectarines. I was about four years old and I was with my sister walking through these rows of stone fruit. I remember feeling very happy and very free."

While Alex remembers this as a happy time, Sylvia has other memories. It was around this time that she was consulting doctors and therapists in an effort to determine what was wrong with her son. He refused to sleep and he was very destructive. For example, he would go around pulling pot plants out of their pots. He would also bash his head on the tiles. "I would just stand there and cry," remembers Sylvia.

The first paediatrician she consulted, when Alex was three, told Sylvia her son was naughty and to take him home and smack him if he misbehaved. "He said when you're out in public don't do it so much, because you'll get reported. I said to him, 'how do you smack a child who does not acknowledge they are being disciplined?' If I ever did give him one on the bottom he would just look up at me. If I screamed at him, he'd just look up at me. It wasn't right. The doctor said to bring him back in a year and we'll throw him on some medication and we'll take it from there. I was devastated. It was horrible. We didn't go back.

"So we just plodded through. If I had to work outside Alex would come along with me. If we had visitors he would lock himself in the bedroom. He was sharing a bedroom with Carlo and me because there were six of us living in a three-bedroom house. One time, when he was about five, I came in and found baby powder everywhere, all over my bed, all over the TV, all over the room. I was vacuuming the living room and I'm ashamed to say it but I grabbed the vacuum cleaner hose and I ran after him shouting 'I will kill you!' I realised at that point that I'd snapped and had to do something about this."

Just before Alex was due to start preschool Sylvia took him to a different paediatrician, whom she says has "pretty much been our savior through all of this". While the paediatrician didn't diagnose Alex at this stage, she gave Sylvia some coping strategies. Sylvia had very little time to herself, as Alex was very clingy and refused to be looked after by anyone else. She had always had short hair, but it grew long because she could not find time alone to go to the hairdresser. Juggling the needs of Alex and her other children, she felt frayed at the edges, so she decided to put Alex in preschool. But it was tough. He would scream when Sylvia left in the morning. When she came to pick him up at the end of the day, she would find him hyperventilating in the cot. The teachers reported that he wasn't mixing with the other children and he didn't grasp some basic concepts. He was slower when it came to talking. And this became more pronounced when he started kindergarten at the local Catholic school.

"One day the school rang me and told me that they'd had to clear the class out," recalls Sylvia. "Another kid had knocked down Alex's tower of building blocks and he'd gone ballistic. They had to call the special education teacher in and clear all the other kids out while he had a meltdown."

Upon the advice of the school, Sylvia organised for an autism consultant named Freda to observe Alex in class. At the end of the day, the consultant concluded, "he's got autism and I'm afraid he's got it good." Sylvia was shocked and confounded. The only thing she had ever heard about autism was bad. "I said no, no, no. Autistic kids don't talk. They don't function."

On the upside, the consultant observed that the girls in Alex's class rubbed his back when he became stressed or upset. He had good support in the other children. Sylvia took to researching autism in books and online, at a time—the early 2000s—when information was not as readily available as it is now. Before long, she started lending her books to Alex's doctors. "I went to one doctor and explained Alex's situation and he said 'Asperger's? What's that?'" Meanwhile, Freda the autism consultant continued to be Sylvia's source of erudite advice. "I rang her one day after watching Alex continuously bash his head on the tiles. She said 'you can either get him a helmet or ignore it'. I thought I couldn't sit and watch a kid with a helmet bashing his head so I ignored him and after a couple of weeks it stopped. Those two weeks were tough."

I am reminded of Barry M. Prizant's book *Uniquely Human*, where he writes that people on the spectrum do things for a reason, and rather than look at the behaviour as "random, deviant or bizarre, as many professionals have called it for decades" we, as parents and teachers and friends, need to question "why?".[41] Prizant writes: "There is no such thing as autistic behavior. These are all *human* behaviors and *human* responses based on a person's experience."[42] Rather than focus on the behaviour itself, it is important to consider the 'why' behind the behaviour.

When Alex was banging his head, he may have been feeling overwhelmed and frustrated, or may have been having difficulty communicating his needs. It is difficult to know, but there was a reason for his response. Of course, as a mother, Sylvia felt frightened that her son might hurt himself. She also felt very confused. Her daughter and step-son had not exhibited such behaviour and it scared her. While the advice "Just ignore it and it will go away" worked on this occasion, it didn't answer her niggling fears and confusion. It also went against the parenting advice of her Italian mother-in-law for example, who felt that children should be scolded for 'misbehaviour'. But was it really 'misbehaviour'? Looking back now she realises that Alex was struggling with feelings of anxiety. It was just so hard to read at the time. Sylvia tried to understand. She poured over books. She spoke to whomever she could. But still the answers were elusive. She felt so very alone.

Sylvia did find some solace in a support group of other parents from Alex's school who also had children on the spectrum. The group was organised by one of the teachers, who had lost her own son to drugs. "We looked at her situation and I think it lifted us out of our own worlds," Sylvia says. "We realised that we were actually lucky. Our children were alive, very alive, and they were gorgeous in their own way. So we were thankful. And we could also talk to each other about our situations."

Sylvia, at least, no longer felt so isolated. But acceptance was not so easily forthcoming. She became side-tracked with finding a 'cure'; taking Alex to a Chinese herbalist, a naturopath, a chiropractor, and trialling ADHD medication for a couple of years, until he refused at around age 12 because it made him feel depressed. "We plodded through and plodded through. And eventually, finally, found some level of acceptance. Over time I also learnt to 'save my battles'."

She remembers how worried she was in the early days: "When they are at a young age you can't see a future ahead. I spent the early years worrying that he was never going to get ahead. I used to think that he'd never know what it was like to have a partner, or a family of his own. But as he's getting older I can see a very good future."

Prizant concurs:

> It's hard for parents raising a child with autism to have perspective. Mothers and fathers are often so caught up in the day-to-day demands of parenting that they can easily forget that whatever is happening now represents just a single moment in time.
>
> When a child seems stuck in a pattern of troubling or perplexing behavior, it can be difficult to imagine her ever progressing further...What causes so much stress for people with autism also induces stress for parents: uncertainty—in this case, about the future...It's important to remember that people with autism progress through developmental stages just as we all do...And no two journeys are alike.[43]

Alex also remembers the early years as being particularly difficult. For one, he found school frustrating and confusing.

"Primary school was really tough. I really disliked it. High school years weren't really any better. I just wanted to be a chameleon and blend in with the furniture wherever I went. I practically went through the first three years of high school years unseen, unknown.

"I was a very shy, nervous kid, very quiet. I had three friends I was close to and I was just that quiet kid. My friends were in different classes of course, so class time was pretty tough going. I found some social things hard to understand. And learning was difficult too.

"It probably wasn't until the last two years of high school that I started enjoying school and then of course you graduate and get out into the real world, and you discover that work is just as hard. In fact school is an absolute bludge compared to work, although I try to be rational about it and learn new things every day."

One area he feels he is constantly improving upon through work is communication. Being a barista and market salesman would require a honed level of social aptitude that anyone would find demanding, let alone someone on the autism spectrum.

"I'd be lying if I said it wasn't a challenge. Geez it's hard," laughs Alex. "I'm exhausted by the end of the day. I'm also a very literal personal. Sometimes when people place their coffee order, I sometimes have to double guess or I correct certain things. Like when someone says 'I'll have this coffee with one sweetener, I might ask them 'do you mean sugar or Equal?' because they're both sweeteners."

Alex's sister Vanessa says that her brother's social skills have vastly improved over the years and that he is a genuine asset to the family business. But while the siblings have a good relationship now, they used to fight incessantly. She remembers some very stressful times.

"We didn't really have the easiest upbringing," she says. "Aside from Alex's autism, there's the reality of farming. If hail hits then it wipes out not only the crops, but also the year's finances. Added to that was the reality of living with my dad's mother. She was a very strict Italian woman, with strong traditional views. Everyone was always on edge, but at the same time we knew that our parents loved us and we were supported as individuals. Just as Alex and I are different, so is our older brother. And I think that was really important that we all were treated differently and not just thrown into the one basket."

I think back to an autism conference that I attended some years back, and a presenter who spoke about the challenges of having a sibling with autism. She discussed how much she hated having her autistic brother at school with her, how she felt embarrassed and was labelled as '*his* sister'. She did say, however, that the experience made her a better person—more empathic and less judgmental.

Vanessa, who works in recruitment, says having Alex in her life has helped her develop a greater understanding and awareness of people's idiosyncrasies. "I feel that I'm able to identify people, without them necessarily telling me they have a disability such as autism," she explains. "I think it's changed me as a person, for the better. I'd like to think I'm more understanding and sensitive to those kinds of people."

Five years and five days apart in age, Alex and Vanessa were only at school together for a year or so. Interestingly, it is Alex who talks about having to follow in the footsteps of Vanessa and her 'rebellious ways'. Vanessa, meanwhile, says her attitude to Alex straddled those of protective mother and annoyed sister.

"We had one year in primary school together," she says. "I was in Year Six and he was in Year One. I remember all the kids were lining up for the canteen and Alex walked straight up to the front of the line. Some kid grabbed him by the collar and I stepped in and shouted 'hey, leave my brother alone'."

At home, however, Vanessa was less nurturing, especially when she attempted to retreat to her room for some space. "He would knock on the door saying 'let me in, let me in'. I wanted privacy and was protective of my own things. There was this one time when he got in and went nuts with red lipstick all over my dressing table and mirror and it was very frustrating, to say the least. We'd often get into punch-ups, like normal siblings do, I suppose."

While her parents spoke to Vanessa about Alex's autism, she doesn't remember having much understanding around the topic. As far as she was concerned, Alex was just Alex and as a teenage girl, she had her own emotional rollercoaster to contend with.

"Mum gave me a very thin book on Asperger's once. I don't know if it was sibling-specific but I remember the advice was to be patient, and to be an upstanding individual. But it didn't really help me to deal with how I was feeling. It's hard for another child. It's almost like Alex and I have a love-hate relationship. I was the protective sister, but I also fought with him because I was the only one who could have a go at him, no one else could. I was kind of conscious of being a normal sibling to him, because I knew that the real world wouldn't be so forgiving.

"Then I'd have my grandmother in my ear. If Alex and I did get into an argument, in her broken English she would say, 'he's sick, he's sick, leave him alone'. That used to bug me. I used to say, 'he's not sick! Yes, he has autism, but that's just who he is'. I sometimes felt misunderstood. While my grandmother would feel for him, I would think 'where is the understanding for me? He just attacked my bedroom with red lipstick! Let me be angry!'" Again, I am reminded of Prizant, who writes:

Autism isn't an illness. It's a different way of being human. Children with autism aren't sick; they are progressing through developmental stages as we all do. To help them we don't need to change them or fix them. We need to work to understand them, and then change what *we* do.

In other words, the best way to help a person with autism change for the better is to change ourselves—our attitudes, our behavior, and the type of support we provide.[44]

Vanessa, now 27, says it is important siblings attempt to understand their brother or sister, but also acknowledge their own emotions. "My advice to siblings is not to beat themselves up if they do get frustrated at times. It's a natural emotion. It doesn't make you a bad person. There were times when I'd think 'I must be more patient'. Yes, accept your sibling for who they are, but also accept yourself for who you are. Try and be understanding and see things from their perspective, but recognise you're not a superhuman being. You don't know everything and nor will you cope appropriately in every situation."

In recent years, Alex and Vanessa's relationship has evolved into friendship. They tried living together for a while, but living separately is a more amenable arrangement. Vanessa recalls helping Alex with job-hunting when he first decided to become a barista. "I guess he doesn't have the same sort of drive that I have, for example. So, having the best of intentions, I would push him a little, and then a little more in an effort to help him to be more independent. One day I wrote a page-long list of places where he could drop off his CV, along with directions. He got lost on the way and rang me really flustered. Then he cracked the shits and turned around and came home and didn't want to speak to me. He just wanted to be left alone to watch TV or play on his computer or be lost in his own world. I probably pushed it a bit far and it backfired on this occasion."

Renowned author Temple Grandin, herself on the autism spectrum, has written about the role family and professionals can play in 'pushing' people with autism in order to learn vital life skills. In *The Loving Push*, co-written by Debra Moore, she writes about the important role her mother played in teaching her how to socialise and carry out basic everyday skills:

> Mother knew that she had to 'stretch' and lovingly push me just outside my comfort zone so I could develop to my fullest. She was always urging me to try new things but she made sure there were no surprises, because a sudden introduction of something new was scary.[45]

Grandin goes on to write that many children on the spectrum are ill-prepared for adulthood because their parents have overprotected them and not allowed them opportunities to do things on their own. This includes everything from household chores to part-time work, or even letting kids speak up for themselves. As Vanessa (and I) can attest, the 'loving push' can sometimes backfire, and at times a careful, gentle guiding hand on the receiver's own terms is what is required. Grandin writes: "Mother had a natural instinct and knew how to stretch me in increments without causing too much stress."[46] I know from experience that too much pushing can result in an explosion, while too little means never moving forward.

I am impressed at how independent, sociable and skillful Alex is at age 22. It's hard to imagine my own son holding down a full-time job that involves relating to customers day in, day out. But perhaps he would be fine. Perhaps I don't give him enough credit. For Alex, I'm sure that working on the farm and in the markets from an early age would have helped, as would have Sylvia and Carlo's parenting decisions. Doing a job that he enjoys and living independently, Alex is carving out a hopeful future for himself. Beyond that, he is personable and speaks lovingly about his family. He seems extremely kind and empathic. As I interview him, my mind keeps darting back to my own boy and speaking with Alex reassures me no end. But there's no denying it's hard work for all involved, particularly in the younger years.

"He was talking the other day," says Sylvia "and said, 'Mum, when I get a girlfriend I'm going to get her name tattooed on my chest'. I said, 'son, girls come and go, but I'll always be your mother. Why don't you get a tattoo that says *Mum*?' We had a good laugh.

"A few years back I used to worry that if something happened to me, what would happen to him? But now I could die happy knowing that my son is going to be a good member of society.

"You've just got to be positive and take each day as it comes. Each day is a different day. And you just have to say to yourself I'm doing the best that I can and that's all you can do. If you know in your heart you've done the best you can, that's all your child or anyone can ask for."

The soprano

Liesel & Susan

When Liesel sat her oral exams for a university degree in Operatic Performance, she requested the examiners move her to a larger room. Liesel has acutely sensitive hearing, and in the smaller room she could hear all of the piano's harmonics, rather than the individual notes she was supposed to be focusing on. She also felt claustrophobic and had difficulty breathing in the confined space, and therefore, had difficulty singing. Thankfully, Liesel had developed an awareness of her sensory needs over time and could articulate these to her examiners, who kindly obliged.

Some years on, not only has she graduated with Bachelor and Postgraduate degrees in Classical Music, but the now 26-year-old has applied for a scholarship to study her Masters in Opera in

Germany and Italy. Her love of musical theatre began at an early age, when her mother took her to see a production of *Phantom of the Opera*. It touched a raw nerve in her and she went home begging to start singing lessons. From that point on, she knew what she wanted to do with her life. Fast forward, and she has realised her dream, now keeping up with a steady stream of mezzo-soprano roles within Australia, including the lead of Dame Nellie in a recent production of *Melba*.

Liesel and I meet mid-afternoon at a suburban Chinese restaurant in Perth. Funnily enough, the restaurant is not far from where I grew up. It is not a place I would chose to go to for coffee, but it is one that Liesel finds familiar and comfortable. Looking all the part of the soprano that she is, and too glamorous for such a modest venue, her diva curves fill her figure-hugging burgundy dress, her dark hair is long and silken, and her make-up is freshly applied. We greet with a hug, despite this being our first ever face-to-face meeting. I spoke to Liesel on the telephone a year ago and was taken aback by how articulate she was, more so than many neurotypical people I have interviewed over the phone. Looking back, I think I was expecting an awkward, stilted conversation, knowing Liesel was on the autism spectrum. But my predetermined judgments were wrong, again, and the conversation left me wanting to put a face to the voice. Today's meeting has taken many text messages and emails to organise, our exchanges becoming more casual over time. As she sits opposite me, a TV blaring in one corner of the restaurant and the sounds of washing-up and clattering cutlery coming from the kitchen, I feel like I am with an old acquaintance.

The first thing I get Liesel to do is to sign a consent form giving me permission to write her story, as I have done with all of the interview subjects in this project. She has been promising to post the form back to me following our phone interview, but has failed to do so, even after my persistent badgering.

"I am so sorry," she blurts out. "I am notoriously disorganised. I have to take some other paperwork to the post office, but I just can't seem to get there. I freeze up every time I think about it. I don't know what it is about me and paperwork."

"That's OK," I reply. "Formalities are out of the way now."

Being disorganised or having difficulty with 'executive functions' is a trait many people on the spectrum struggle with, especially those with the often-accompanying condition of ADHD. Executive functions are the skills needed to make a plan and carry it out. They include working memory, which controls the many things our brain can juggle at any given moment; prospective memory, or remembering to actually do tasks in the future (whether that be in five minutes or in an hour); problem solving; planning and sequencing; having a sense of time and time management; persistence; and transitioning between one activity and another.[47] Add to this the difficulty that someone on the spectrum may have with regulating emotions, and it can be concluded that 'simple' tasks may not be that simple at all.

Despite such challenges, Liesel lives independently on the other side of the country to her family, has several part-time jobs, a partner, and has recently bought a car. She moved when she successfully auditioned and was accepted into the performing arts program at her university. The ensuing years were a heady mix of music productions, classes, friendships and jobs to pay the rent—stints as a make-up artist, model, babysitter and children's entertainer (specialising in Disney princesses). And then there was study, which she has always struggled with, even in primary school, when she led a petition to abolish homework.

"As an adult I don't have many of the socially inhibiting aspects of autism but the main thing I still struggle with is compartmentalisation," she explains. "School is for study, home is for other things. When I was at university, if I wanted to do singing practice for a part, or anything uni-related, I'd have to literally drive there to do it. Home is my downtime."

This is common among students on the spectrum, who are exhausted after applying themselves both academically and socially all day long. I think of Tom, who has always been black and white about the homework issue, although thankfully he's coming around to the concept of study, as long as it's a subject he enjoys. When the school bell goes at three o'clock it clearly signals the end of the day. He's out that door, see you later, there's no looking back. He just wants to come home and relax. His school offers an after-school homework club in the library, but I gave up trying to get Tom to go there after my second attempt. "It's called HOME work for a reason Mum and the answer is no way," he clearly stated. The challenge, of course, is getting the HOME work done at home.

For Liesel, the need to categorise, or separate her interests, affects many aspects of her life. "I get really stressed if I have to mix my circles of friends, for example," she says. "If I have to introduce my friends from uni to my friends from work, I sort of push it away and avoid it."

Such anxieties play a daily role in her life. She says she still has meltdowns, often misinterpreted throughout her childhood as tantrums. Thankfully, her boyfriend now recognises when her tensions are rising and tries not to take it personally. This has taken some explanation on Liesel's part and compassion on his. Liesel is very open about her autism and explained early on that she sometimes became overwhelmed and needed time out.

"I kind of lose volume control," Liesel says. "A meltdown is when everything sort of gets too much. It's a feeling of not being able to cope. I guess it's probably similar to having a panic attack, but it displays in a different way. When I'm having a meltdown I tend to lash out, which of course I don't mean, but it can be hard for the people around me."

Liesel wasn't always so aware of how her emotions played out, both internally and externally. She is frank when she says that school was "very, very tough". Diagnosed with Asperger's at age 13, shortly after her father's Asperger's diagnosis, Liesel struggled socially and in class. While many neurotypical teens struggle with negotiating friendships, those on the spectrum face added challenges and difficulties in understanding the complexities of social interaction. This can in turn affect self-esteem and compound anxiety. Add to this a limited capacity for flexibility and a low frustration threshold and the results can be "explosive", in the words of clinical child psychologist Ross W. Greene. He writes that many differently wired children have: "[t]he tendency to think in a concrete, rigid, black and white manner. The child does not recognise the grey in many situations ("Mrs Robinson is *always* mean! I *hate* her!" rather than

"Mrs Robinson is usually nice, but she was in a really bad mood today"); may apply oversimplified, rigid, inflexible rules to complex situations; and may impulsively revert to such rules even when they are obviously inappropriate."[48]

Subsequently, Liesel often felt "backed into a corner" and her coping mechanism was combative. She became a goth and was regularly placed on detention or suspended from school for truancy and misbehavior. When she was in Year 10, a school guidance officer told her she needn't bother pursuing subjects for the mainstream leaving certificate, as she would never go to university. "Ha! I wish he could see me now," she laughs. "I have to admit though that I was a total ratbag. School was a really difficult time. I didn't understand the other kids and they didn't understand me. So I just rebelled. I would have meltdowns and become very down. I also learned to be funny and used that as a bit of a shield through my adolescence."

Liesel has four older siblings, and the closest in age is seven years older than her, and so, she says, she related very well to adults, but not other children. She also had difficulty dealing with the dynamic of student-teacher relationships, namely with teachers as authority figures.

"I didn't really see myself as rebellious, because I didn't understand what the situation was," says Liesel.

"I was just being myself. I didn't understand that my behaviour and the way I talked was wrong. I also didn't understand that I wasn't an adult. I had trouble making friends my own age. I wasn't interested in the things that they were interested in. I didn't understand the dynamics of being a 13 year old girl."

While her diagnosis helped the teachers to understand Liesel's quirks, she says that in many ways, it made her feel more alienated at an age when all a teenager wants is to fit in. She also struggled with following instructions in class. While some teachers 'scaffolded' her work, most of the time she wouldn't know where to start or what was expected of her. The thing that eventually saved her was changing schools. "Things got a lot better when I moved to a performing arts school with like-minded kids. There, we were expected to take responsibility for our own actions. We weren't expelled for not turning up to class; it just meant that we didn't learn. And by that stage I was engaged enough with the lessons that I wanted to learn."

It was at this school that Liesel met her first boyfriend. He too had a passion for classical music and after finishing school, he moved to London to study opera. They were together for four years, and it was at his insistence that Liesel applied to study at university. The long-distance relationship was not to last, but they still stay in touch.

Liesel's mother Susan says her youngest daughter was an "interesting child", precocious and willful. "She wasn't always as delightful as she is now," Susan laughs. "She was a gorgeous child, but definitely difficult. She was very forthright when she felt any of her friends were not being justly treated. Right from the time she was in prep [kindergarten], she was very outspoken and the teachers didn't really know what to make of her. She more or less considered herself to be a midget adult. She thought she had the same rights as everybody else, just that she was a little bit smaller."

Susan remembers how hard it was, before she realised that Liesel had sensory difficulties and what a meltdown actually was. These days, Susan is an expert. "When a child is having a 'tantrum' they are knowingly manipulating their parents or carer," she explains. "Conversely, when a child is having a 'meltdown' they are totally out of control. So although they both appear very similar, the motivation is different. If you walk out of a room when a child is having a tantrum, they'll quite often stop. When a child is having a meltdown, they're not aware of their actions."

As Ross W. Greene explains, by the time the child has reached meltdown stage, they have lost their "capacity for, coherent, rational thought". There is no point in attempting to educate or scold them as "little or no learning occurs for a child while he is in the midst of a meltdown."[49] It wasn't until Liesel's diagnosis that Susan knew what she was grappling with. She learnt to become more flexible with her approach. Conversely, she came to realise why Liesel was so inflexible, why she was so literal, why there was no room for sarcasm or satire. She also learnt to give Liesel more space. "Life got so much easier because my expectations were put in sync with Liesel's processing skills. I also learnt to understand triggers and to keep the stress levels down."

Susan now realises all five of her adult children are probably somewhere on the autism spectrum, as is her ex-husband. Each one of them is immensely artistic, with three of them classically trained in music. Two of Susan's grandchildren have also been diagnosed with autism. "They are such individual, talented, wonderful people that I don't quite know how I would have coped with kids who weren't on the spectrum," she says. "A lot of parents think it's the worst thing that ever happened to me, but in actual fact it's not. I just love their individuality and creativity."

She feels immensely proud of all her children's accomplishments, including those of her youngest, Liesel. "She was always rather an independent little body, although perhaps more independent in her mind than she was actually capable of being. She manages on what little money she makes. She's bought a car. She pays her rent. She makes me very proud. I'm very close to her and she still likes to hop into bed with me and we watch television together."

Susan describes how her experience with her own children and her subsequent understanding of autism has strengthened her relationship with her grandchildren. Formerly a teacher, she also feels it broadened her understanding of her students. When she was working as a relief teacher, she could pick the child with ASD within about 20 minutes of being in the classroom with them. "I found that advantageous because I was able to work with a child who would normally create a lot of angst for a temporary teacher. I knew they would have a hot button and were behaving in a certain way because of certain challenges and yet I was able to get their confidence and their cooperation. It's been good for me in that sense."

Susan describes how she might talk to children showing signs of stress and frustration: "I say to them, 'when you're starting to feel stressed what does your tummy feel like? What do your hands feel like? What does your head feel like?' I try and get them to identify these feelings so that as they get older they have coping strategies to be able to either remove themselves from the situation or do something to bring down the level of stress."

I remark that Susan's advice has boded well with Liesel, who is obviously very aware of her stress triggers as an adult. "We had a few problems for a while there though," Susan says. "During her teens I didn't factor in a lot of her mindset. Once my ex-husband was diagnosed he was able to say to me, 'Look, this is why she's feeling this way and you don't really understand because you don't have the same mindset.' I could then see where I fell down with her and with the other kids, Liesel's older siblings, but now, I think with the grandkids, I'm right on top of it."

As she speaks, I can't help but think that Susan is being hard on herself (like most mothers, myself included). Later, when I look at my interview notes, I have written, "What an amazing human!" I think of the amount of time that she has invested in her five children, her grandchildren, her students and her ex-husband. She even left work for a year to care for her ex-mother-in-law, who had dementia. I marvel at Susan's patience. She doesn't appear to be at all resentful. Yet she feels a sense of guilt for not doing enough and for not attending to Liesel's needs earlier and more effectively. I have written: "How could she have done more!" in the column of my notes. "Five children on the spectrum!" I can't imagine.

While all of her own children have grown up and left home, Susan still lives with her ex-husband in the family home. They separated about six months before he was diagnosed. He had moved to the country and heard Tony Attwood, the Asperger's expert, speaking on the television. He rang Susan in tears of relief and shock and sadness, coming to grips with his condition. "We separated because I felt lonely and unable to manage the relationship," she explains. "I would have liked to have known about the Asperger's beforehand, but this wasn't the case and I think it just went on too long for me to handle it. I now realise I wasn't just handling one Aspie, I was handling a whole family of them." Despite the lack of a formal commitment, she still considers that she and her ex-husband will grow old together and she will care for him the rest of their days. "I don't consider him my husband. But funnily enough we probably get along better now," she says. "There's no pressure for him to be someone he's not."

I am struck by Susan's generosity and selflessness. It is like she knows no other role other than the one of carer and as far as I'm concerned, she is a saint. A saint, that is, with mother-guilt. It is a common thread in so many stories I have come across, where it is the mother who acts as a guide and teacher. Liesel has never had therapy, other than the psychology she had as a child before she was diagnosed. Instead, Susan has taught Liesel many of the skills she has needed in life. Liesel also spent a lot of time with her maternal grandmother, who was an elocution special-ist. That explains her beautiful articulation over the phone and in person.

With a background in musical theatre, Susan directed Liesel in a production of *Carousel* and noticed her lack of eye contact with fellow cast members when she was on stage. When Liesel and I meet, one of the first things I notice are her beautiful eyes and long eyelashes. I also notice how good her eye contact is.

"Her eyes are so obvious on her face," says Susan. "She was playing the lead role and it was noticeable to the audience when she didn't look other characters in the eye. I would keep reminding her and keep reminding her until she got it right. She has very good eye contact in general conversation now, but I notice she still looks away when she's stressed. Of course up on stage she's concentrating and there is a degree of stress."

Liesel also remembers her mother's persistence: "Up until the age of 19, I could not make eye contact. I didn't even realise I was doing it until my mother pointed it out. We sort of had a staring contest and she'd tell me when I was looking away because I honestly didn't realise that I was either looking over someone's head or looking just to the side of their face. It was something we spent a lot of time on together. My mother persevered and, well, as you can imagine, I wasn't happy about it at the time. She was tough."

Perseverance, from both mother and child, is a sentiment that echoes through much of what Liesel says. "For people on the spectrum who want to make positive changes in their life, it's just about hard work and accepting the things you want to change. It's about working at it and never being ashamed to ask for help."

While Liesel feels she has a natural affinity for music and memorising lyrics and musical scores, she also admits her ability to focus on what she loves has helped. In the autism world, this could be classified as a 'special' or 'deep interest', 'enthusiasm' or "bordering on obsession" as Liesel puts it. The rewards for focussing on an interest can be immense and can define a career. And I would presume that such "obsession" is almost necessary if a person is to make it in the world of classical music. It is apparent that Liesel has focus, but she has also worked hard to reach her career goals. She has put in the hours of practice and study needed to succeed.

Her passion for performing started early in life, and was reinforced by her family's shared love of singing: "My father sang sort of professionally and my siblings sang, but I decided I wanted to start singing when I was eight. I went to see *Phantom of the Opera*, which of course isn't an opera, but it sort of inspired my love for music and I did do a lot of music theatre in my teens. I started doing opera seriously when I was about 16 or 17."

I immediately think of the Phantom of the Opera, Erik, who wears a mask to hide his disfigurement and of Christine, with whom he falls in love and whom he kidnaps in the hope that she will eventually love him back for who he is. Perhaps it wasn't just the music that appealed to a young Liesel, but the story too.

"I do find opera and musical theatre very moving," she says. "I find the stories very beautiful and touching and sort of, hyper-realistic. I like the display of emotion. Classical music in particular speaks to me in a way that a lot of other music doesn't. I'm quite an emotional person and music plays to that."

I find Liesel's connection to the emotional side of musical narrative quite telling. It contrasts with the traditional belief that people with autism show immaturity when it comes to understanding and expressing emotion. Hans Asperger wrote in 1944, "The children cannot be understood simply in terms of the concept 'poverty of emotion' used in a quantitative sense. Rather what characterises these children is a qualitative difference, a disharmony in emotion and disposition".[50] It's not that they are emotionless, or feel less. It could actually be that they feel more intensely. Indeed, the incidence of mood disorders in people on the spectrum could be indicative of this. Attwood writes: "The degree of expression of negative emotions such as anger, anxiety and sadness can be extreme, and described by parents as an on/off switch set at maximum volume".[51]

I know that Tom is very quick to pick up on the mood of a situation. While he might not be able to read body language or social cues as accurately as a neurotypical person, he can certainly pick up on the 'vibe', as unscientific as that sounds. When we were visiting San Francisco we took a walk through Haight-Ashbury, known of course for its role in '60s hippie culture, fashion and music. These days, sadly, it is also known for its junkies and homelessness. Funnily enough, James and I were too excited to notice the number of people who were 'out of it'. Our adult filters blocked out what we didn't want to see or feel, but for Tom it was too much. He felt uneasiness in his very core, to the point where he felt nauseous. Thankfully, my friend was on hand to take him to a nearby park to rebalance the sensory overload, take a few deep breaths and calm him down, while James and I continued to shop.

According to Susan, this ability to feel more intensely relates to the way that children on the spectrum feel empathy. Contrary to theories that describe autistics as lacking empathy, she believes they feel so much emotion it is overwhelming—the same way they may be hypersensitive to stimuli such as sight, taste, hearing, touch or smell. Sensory Integration Dysfunction is common among people on the spectrum and hypersensitivity is one of the ways it can manifest. A child in this situation might avoid or run away from the loud sound that is hurting his or her ears, or place a barrier between themselves and the sound. They may appear aggravated or irritable.[52] Susan believes that empathy can be thought of in a similar way. At a parent workshop I recently attended, we were asked to go around the room and say what we each loved about our child on the spectrum. Interestingly, a large proportion of parents said they loved that their child was so empathic and sensitive to others' emotions. Interesting, because it butts up against stereotypes that suggest otherwise.

"My experience is that these children can empathise, they can most certainly empathise," says Susan. "But they actually have to shut off in some cases because they identify so strongly that it becomes sensory overload. They have to pull back because it is too much. They feel the tension and distress of another person to the point it becomes, like the hearing is, acute. The sense of hearing, of taste, their sense of smell, all of these things are acute. So is their sense of distress. Their emotional surroundings might be extreme too and so they protect themselves by putting up a barrier."

I think Susan has a point. Barry M. Prizant writes: "When some people with autism encounter strong emotions in people—happiness, sadness, excitement, nervousness—they become confused. It's as if they are absorbing the intensity of the emotions themselves, without understanding why they feel as they do."[53]

For Liesel, such waves of emotion still regularly strike, but she can generally reach into her toolbox of coping strategies to get her through. Sometimes though, it does get too much. "I do struggle with anxiety a lot and relationships, because it's very difficult to be understood and sometimes that can get really depressing."

As much as her parents have showered her with unconditional love, she says friendships and romantic relationships are a different story. I ask Liesel if she ever imagines what life would be like if she were not on the spectrum.

"More so than wondering what it would be like to be neurotypical, I sometimes dream about being in a world of finding someone who really understands me and of being accepted, completely, for who I am. I do try and have a bit of neurotypical empathy when it comes to my mother. I try and imagine how she feels sometimes, but I don't think I've ever really thought about what my life would be like if I were neurotypical."

And that's when I realise how arrogant it is of me to presume that Liesel would want to change, when it is really the people around her who need to change and to be more understanding. Liesel is who she is, and like all of us, she strives for connection with others. Strangely, I feel an instant empathy toward Liesel. I find her warm and open and funny, and throughout our conversation I find myself constantly wiping away tears. But I also wonder how much of her true self she is stifling or hiding from me.

Perhaps it is her experience in theatre, or the many years of honing her social skills on friends and siblings. Perhaps, in part, it is also because she is female and females are notoriously good at hiding their autism, or 'masking'. Tony Attwood writes: "I have noted that girls with Asperger's syndrome may be more difficult to recognise and diagnose due to coping and camouflaging mechanisms".[54] He writes that girls on the spectrum are more inclined to observe the social interactions of other children and after gathering up their research, then carry out their play as if it comes intuitively. Rather, they are using their intellect. Girls may also be more inconspicuous because they politely decline invitations to join in. Other girls too, can be maternal, forgiving and understanding. A study in *Autism Research* (2017) approaches things from a different perspective.[55] The study, which incorporated interviews with parents of 79 females and 158 males on the spectrum, suggests that girls have more difficulty with executive function and daily living skills. Such skills might translate to tasks such as cleaning, meeting appointments, managing finances or, for instance, Liesel's aversion to paperwork. Nevertheless, she is most definitely 'making it' in a neurotypical world.

When Liesel and I bid farewell I get the sense that this will not be the last time we meet. I wish her good luck with her plans to move to Europe. "It's a scary prospect," she says. "But so is everything until you do it." We leave the Chinese restaurant and, squinting into the Western Australian afternoon sun, I watch Liesel drive down the Canning Highway, a road I know well from my formative Perth years. I wipe away stray tears, and I ponder what her next chapter might entail.

Shifting perspectives

Not surprisingly, most of the parents I interviewed for this project had a relatively limited knowledge of autism when their children were first diagnosed. What they did know was largely drawn from cultural representations. Over time, however, through research and lived experience, these parents have become semi-experts. Not only do they intimately understand their own children, but they also grasp the politics of autism. They have learnt that there is nothing shameful about autism, and no need for blame, despite historical misconceptions, of which I explore in this chapter. Here, I provide some background on the history of autism to contextualise and better understand current approaches.

Thankfully, the wider public is becoming more versed on the issue. I may be optimistic, but it does seem to me that people are slowly starting to realise that autism is complex and that stereotypes are not helpful. While I can't be sure, I want to say that the world is becoming an easier place to live for people on the spectrum, and their families, largely due to increased understanding. The more awareness there is, the less challenging life is for the individual and their families. That is not to say that the difficulties of autism itself go away, but so many obstacles faced by disabled people are socially driven and come from a place of ignorance. As Steve Silberman writes, many of the challenges that people on the spectrum face are not "'symptoms' of their autism, but hardships imposed by a society that refuses to make basic accommodations for people with cognitive disabilities."[56] He goes on to say, "The notion that the cure for the most disabling aspects of autism will never be found in a pill, but in supportive communities, is one that parents have been coming to on their own for generations."[57] Supportive kinships, and shared stories, help to show that we needn't talk about autism in hushed tones. Indeed, stories can offer a pathway to destigmatising disability and making social progress, helping to ensure that myths and *Rain Man*-like labels, such as 'retard' and 'idiot savant', are left behind.

Within the course of researching and writing this book, I have trawled through shelves of books and press clippings. And I am pleased to report that I have noticed an enormous shift in the way that autism is portrayed. When I first started researching, back in the mid-2000s, I would get a sense of excitement if I found an article related to the topic—which is indicative of how little it was discussed back then. Now, it is rare if a day goes by when I don't see something about autism on a news outlet or on social media. It is everywhere, and thankfully I think the topic is being approached with more empathy. This of course is largely due to the growing reach of digital media. Videos and articles are easily shared on Facebook or Twitter, commented on and then passed along to communities worldwide. As long as the message is factual and accurate, this sharing of knowledge can be a wonderful thing.

In her book *Illness as Metaphor*, Susan Sontag writes that some illnesses, such as cancer and HIV/AIDS, are more symbolically charged than others.[58] She writes that by using metaphors and stereotypes we blame the sufferer for contracting the disease and not being strong enough to overcome it. While autism is not an illness, it too has been charged with metaphor and misunderstanding. Despite the great progress that has been made, there is still stigma surrounding autism and around difference. One only has to look at the way the

Andrew Wakefield vaccine scare played out when parents were blamed for causing autism by trying to prevent their children from contracting measles, mumps and rubella—and the subsequent guilt and shame they unjustly suffered. I recently witnessed the remnants of this campaign when a mother verbally attacked me in the park, insisting that the "autism epidemic" was caused by parents vaccinating their children, after I told her the topic of my book. Although shaken by her aggression, I was not surprised by her misguided thinking. Despite experts like Tony Attwood steadfastly insisting that autism is "not caused by inadequate parenting or psychological or physical trauma",[59] these ill-conceived notions still linger.

In Australia, the parent-run organisation Autism Awareness advocates for autism through a combination of articles on social media, events and broadcast interviews. I attended an event organised by this group in the Utzon Room of the Sydney Opera House, the very room where Tom had his meltdown when a singer in an incy-wincy spider costume leapt from the wings. The audience of practitioners, parents and autistic individuals sipped glasses of champagne, and the event was live-streamed via Facebook. Speakers included hilarious UK Aspie and schoolteacher Chris Bonello, who opened with the line, "Because I'm autistic I'm not supposed to be good at public speaking, or sarcasm for that matter. I apologise if I exceed any expectations." Throughout, I could not help but think how far autism awareness had come, even in the time that I had been involved.

This is also evidenced by the Netflix release of Hannah Gadsby's stand-up show *Douglas*, which has done wonders for increasing awareness of neurodiversity—on a grand scale. Gadsby talks about her recent diagnosis of autism and ADHD on the show, which follows on from her Emmy Award winning show *Nanette*, taking her powerful personal story to millions of people worldwide.

The inclusion of autistic voices, such as Gadsby's and Bonello's, is invaluable. Social media has revolutionised the way self-advocates can help to disrupt unhelpful discourse and hold others accountable when they endeavor to speak on behalf of the neurodiverse community. Indeed that has been top of mind for me in putting together this book and through searching Twitter by using hashtags such as #ActuallyAutistic, I can garner a more informed perspective from some wonderful neurodiverse advocates. Two I have been drawn to are Agonie Autie from the UK and Yenn Purkis from Australia. Purkis told ABC podcast *The Parenting Spectrum*: "Autistic people are not broken neurotypical people. We're valuable, we're who we are and we're fine as we are... Autism is not a curse or a tragedy or a burden. It is a difference."[60] One of the most useful things we can do to understand our children, says Fiona Churchman who produced *The Parenting Spectrum*, is to listen to autistic adults such as Purkis about how they feel. Technology, such as podcasts and social media, is allowing us more opportunity to discover such voices.

As Purkis identifies, the language we use around autism is important, for this frames how it is perceived. In the United States, advocacy groups such as Autism Speaks are being far more cautious about the way they refer to autism. In 2016 the group tweaked the wording of its mission statement and announced it no longer intended to seek a 'cure' for autism spectrum disorder. Words such as 'struggle', 'hardship' and 'crisis' would no longer be present. It's a small change but one that is significant, with author Steve Silberman reportedly stating that the organisation has some "bad karma to burn off". He is referring to the fact that the group had long used metaphors that framed autism as an 'epidemic' or an 'urgent global health crisis'. Such language "understandably terrified parents", said Silberman, and distracted people from the facts.[61]

Of course, it can't be denied that there is still much work to be done, with research showing that children on the spectrum are still at increased risk of bullying.[62] There is also room for improvement when it comes to schools and places of employment. But what is encouraging is that companies such as Google in Silicon

Valley are employing, indeed actively seeking out, people on the spectrum. These companies recognise that employees on the spectrum think differently and have an innate capacity to focus, despite their possibly limited social abilities. Such themes were explored in the 2018 and 2019 ABC TV series *Employable Me* (based on the 2016 BBC series of the same name). "I'm glad you can make use of my weapons-grade autism", laughed jobseeker Jonathon in the series. He had landed a competitive paid internship, channeling his passion for accountancy. As well as a love of numbers, he boasted a wicked sense of humour and a way with words. His sentiment is in line with the theme of the series, which promoted harnessing the strengths of its participants, rather than focussing on what they cannot do. Jonathon draws on the metaphor of "a sunflower in a field of poppies" when describing himself and how autism makes him stand out from his job competitors. Indeed he and the other jobseekers profiled in the show are quite remarkable for all of their gifts and abilities.[63]

In the BBC series of *Employable Me*, Professor Baron Cohen states: "People with autism should not be underestimated. They might see things in a fresh way and that could be really valuable in the workplace." The program profiles 34 year old Brett, among others, who has been rejected from the hundreds of jobs he has applied for over the past eight years. Prof. Baron Cohen identifies Brett as being a highly visual learner, a talented piano player and composer, yet he is a poor verbal communicator and did not finish school after being bullied. After sitting for an awkward job interview, an understanding employer gives him a job that involves testing software and he proves to be a whiz with technology. Brett struggles with communicating with fellow employees. In fact, he struggles to be able to say anything to them. Yet he goes on to deliver a speech describing how he finally feels accepted, reducing many of his colleagues, including his boss, to tears.[64]

The success of shows such as *Employable Me* and the 2019 ABC TV series *Love on the Spectrum,* which explored the relationship challenges faced by autistic individuals, indicates that the public is receptive to portrayals of autism that are genuine, or that represent individuals as part of everyday society. Such characters are starting to appear in children's television as well, notably, *Sesame Street's* autistic character Julia. When I told Tom that *Sesame Street* was launching a Muppet with autism, he replied, "Are they even allowed to do that?" He had never seen a character on children's TV who was on the spectrum. He wondered if Julia was taboo or controversial, and his reaction indicated to me that Julia's arrival was long overdue. It turns out Julia is just one of the gang. She has her quirks, taking a while to answer questions, flapping her hands and being sensitive to loud noises. But the other Muppets quickly learn what makes her tick and she is accepted for doing things "just a little differently, in a Julia sort of way." Sesame Workshop, the non-profit organisation behind *Sesame Street*, stated that bullying was a key motivator for the introduction of Julia, and her debut successfully conveys a message of inclusion.[65]

Tom watched the first episode of *Sesame Street* that featured Julia and was heartened by it, identifying with some of Julia's traits, such as being sensitive to sounds. "Elmo's squeaky voice would drive me mad if I were her," he joked. I notice he had a small smile on his face while watching it and afterwards he commented that it was great that shows were becoming more diverse. He told me he was pleased Julia's autism was mentioned, but was not made out to be a big deal. "Autism is simply a part of who she is," Tom told me. He liked the fact that the show was about a group of friends and one of those friends happened to have autism—and this is not something he's seen on TV before. Whereas TV series like *The A-Word,* from the UK, and *Atypical,* from the US, focus on autism as the central theme, *Sesame Street* successfully incorporates autism into the fabric of its diverse community.

I wish that Julia had been introduced when Tom and Otis were toddlers. But her arrival now at least paves the way for more children's characters with autism—allowing children with autism to identify with like-minded characters, and teaching neurotypical kids how to empathically interact with peers on the spectrum. If children can find a little bit of themselves or their friends in characters on the screen or in books, they can see autism from a different perspective. They can see that characters like Julia needn't be taboo or controversial, but rather, merit acceptance and inclusion.

*

Unfortunately, not all representations of autism have been accurate, with many enabling stereotypes. While *Rain Man* substantially raised the profile of autism in 1988, it also reinforced the genius stereotype that remains common today. Meanwhile, back in 1969, the Elvis Presley movie *A Change of Habit* fortified a more damaging myth of its time, the now debunked theory that autism was caused by a mother's inability to bond with her child. Elvis plays the part of a doctor working with underprivileged children in a ghetto clinic. A young girl, abandoned by her mother, is purged of her "autistic frustration" by Dr Elvis as he holds her in a tight embrace.

The 'refrigerator mother' theory came from a child psychiatrist named Leo Kanner, who in fact is credited with 'inventing' autism. Before this, autism was referred to as childhood schizophrenia. Kanner, who was based at John Hopkins Hospital in Baltimore, is widely acclaimed for his progress with autism research and has a reputation as a fairly compassionate clinician, and one who stood up for mental health patients. Many of his ideas around the presentation of his patients are still recognised today, such as a lack of social instinct, an "anxiously obsessive desire for the maintenance of sameness" or "fear of change and surprise".[66] Yet he is also known for the inaccurate assertions that paved the way for the terrible treatment of patients and their parents. Indeed declarations of 'toxic parenting' helped to entrench autism as a source of shame. Such ideas sent research in the wrong direction for decades and the consequences are still felt today. We saw such an example when Australian columnist Andrew Bolt belittled Swedish environmental activist Greta Thunberg, calling her "deeply disturbed".[67] He derided Thunberg's parents for calling her autism a "superpower", writing that "Asperger's or autism are very rarely an advantage". "Who has done this to her?" he wrote of her views on climate change, discrediting her stance as "child abuse".[68] This, of course, is despite (or in spite) of the fact that Thunberg has an international following, was nominated for both the 2019 and 2020 Nobel Peace Prize, and won the Time Person of the Year in 2019.

Kanner did not always blame parents for their children's autism. In fact this assertion was a huge departure from his observations in the early 1940s, when he stated that autism was "innate". He worked tirelessly researching autism for many years, but before playing the 'blame game', did not get any recognition for his work, as Donvan and Zucker write: "Tellingly, it was only after Kanner began talking about children stuck 'in emotional refrigerators' that *Time* magazine wanted to write about autism, and that the rest of the psychiatric field began to take notice".[69]

To give Kanner some credit, he wasn't afraid to admit he'd made a mistake and in 1966 reverted back to his theory about autism being innate. He told an audience, "Herewith I acquit you people as parents"—meaning that the condition was not their fault. But of course by then the damage had been done.[70] Other clinicians, including one by the name of Bruno Bettelheim, had taken up the theory with vigour. In 1967 Bettelheim published a book called *The Empty Fortress*, which essentially reinforced the theory that mothers caused their children's autism.[71] Meanwhile, many young patients were administered vast quantities of drugs, including LSD.[72] The history books are filled with cases of children locked away and tortured by less than sympathetic clinicians. Mothers (and initially fathers too) were psychoanalysed, scrutinised and shunned. The legacy of shame and guilt lasted well beyond Kanner's 'acquittal'.

Around the time that Kanner was discovering autism, another researcher was doing his own observations at the University of Vienna in the midst of Nazi Germany. Hans Asperger gave his first public lecture on autism in 1938 and after extensive research he filed his thesis in October 1943, and published a paper a year later. According to author Steve Silberman, Asperger's paper, published in German against a backdrop of the Holocaust, was virtually ignored for 40 years. In the decades that followed, Asperger was not taken seriously, and instead was criticised for dwelling on the intelligence of his subjects and for the small number of observed cases. Extraordinarily, Silberman writes, Asperger played up the brilliance of his subjects in order to save them from being murdered by the Nazis. At one point, he even suggested to his Nazi superiors that his 'little professors' would make superior code breakers for the Reich. Many of Asperger's patients were less obviously gifted, however, and such children were referred to by German eugenicists as 'useless eaters'. These eugenicists considered that the kindest thing would be to kill them.[73]

In stark contrast to Silberman, author Edith Sheffer suggests Asperger was in fact complicit in the murder of such children. As the Nazi regime sought to eliminate difference from the human race, it targeted children and adults with disabilities, including those who lacked social skills or the ability to follow the masses. Sheffer writes that Asperger's 1938 lecture "appears less a piece of scientific research than a political and social statement... an attempt to navigate the mind-boggling shifts of the Third Reich."[74] While Asperger initially touts the opinion his patients "are not sick", his views change over time and he goes on to believe in assisting National Socialism. In a 1940 talk to the German Society for Pediatrics, Asperger declared that the very purpose of special education was to "align these children with the National Socialist states," a goal of which he "greatly approved".[75] Although Asperger's actions and motives are not clear-cut, Sheffer's research highlights the role that society plays in the development of diagnoses. She concludes that "the history of Asperger and autism should underscore the ethics of respecting every child's mind, and treating those minds with care."[76]

Asperger filed his post doctoral thesis on autistic psychopathy in October 1943, before being drafted into military service and a medical unit in Vienna. Soon after, he was sent to work as a surgeon in a field hospital in Croatia. In 1944, the Children's Clinic at the University of Vienna, where Asperger had conducted his research, was reduced to rubble by Allied bombs. It is believed that Asperger's head nurse, Sister Viktorine, was buried alive with her arms protectively around a young patient. Most of Asperger's work was also lost in the rubble, including the concluding statement of his thesis about "the duty to speak out for these children with the whole force of our personality". Lost too was his theory that autism was "not at all rare" and a "continuum".[77]

This concept was in contrast to Kanner's view that his patients were a strictly defined and monolithic group, not a broad spectrum with widely varying manifestations of their condition. Unlike Asperger's little professors, Kanner downplayed his patients' strengths and saw "no fundamental difference between the eight speaking and the three mute children," for example.[78] Nor did he view autism as a continuum stretching into adulthood, but rather, he focussed on young children only. It wasn't until the 1990s that this view started to diminish—when Asperger's work was officially restored and translated. What a shame so much repair work had to be done.

Kanner and Asperger also differed on their views of parents. While Kanner had taken the view that parents were to blame, Asperger took a decidedly empathic approach. He noticed that many of his patient's parents and grandparents were accomplished, saying "the ancestors of these children have been intellectuals for several generations." Rather endearingly, he noted in one case that both mother and son shared quirks of personality, which gave them a mutual bond: "The mother knew her son through and through and understood his difficulties very well...She tried to find similar traits in herself and in her relations and talked about this eloquently."[79]

The parents seeking advice from Kanner, however, were not admired. Ironically, Silberman writes, the parents were "much like Kanner himself: upper middle-class academics who were savvy and well connected." Silberman continues:

No less than four of the fathers of his original 11 patients were psychiatrists...The mothers of these patients were equally distinguished. In an era when less than one in four women in the United States completed their college education, nine of the mothers had bachelors or graduate degrees. Even the grandparents, aunts, and uncles of these children seemed unusually bright.[80]

Kanner blamed the clever parents for their children's precociousness and their difficulties, saying the parents filled their children's heads with irrelevant nonsense: "He theorised that overambitious parents... had 'stuffed' the impressionable minds of their children with useless information to cast themselves in a culturally favourable light and bolster their own egos."[81] Silberman paraphrases a paper, whereby Kanner writes that "these children had been pushed into mental illness by their selfish, compulsive, and emotionally frosty parents, who tried to substitute poems and symphonies and catechisms and encyclopedias for the nurturing love they were unable to provide."[82] I want to think that such opinions have changed, but again, I am reminded of the haters who accuse Greta Thunberg's parents of manipulation and brainwashing. On the contrary, it would appear that her mother and father are loving and supportive, and Greta's views are her own.[83]

Silberman concludes:

> Where Asperger saw threads of genius and disability inextricably intertwined in his patients' family histories—testifying to the complex genetic roots of their condition and the 'social value of this personality type,' as he put it, Kanner saw the shadow of the sinister figure that would become infamous in popular culture as the 'refrigerator mother'.[84]

The history of autism is teeming with disturbing and confronting moments. I find it difficult to read about the way that people with autism were once treated and were so misunderstood, because I think about

Tom and the people I have interviewed for this book. But facing history is important as it provides insight into how autism has been stigmatised and polarised. It also makes me appreciate how far we have come—how much more awareness there is now and how much support we can draw on. How guilty and demoralised must those mothers, and fathers, have felt? I can't help but put myself in their shoes. I can't help but feel for those parents who were so worried about their children that they took them to specialists, only to be told that they were cold and uncaring. It would have been so distressing. I also have enormous sympathy for the children who were ripped away from their families and often maltreated. Some of those children are now adults, which indicates how recently such institutionalisation occurred.

The irony is that these parents, like the parents interviewed for this project, would have been doing everything in their power to help their children. They went to Kanner for a second, third, fourth opinion, in a bid to understand their child. It is hard to fathom just how terribly they were treated, simply for being themselves and for loving their children, for wanting the best for them. This must have affected their emotional state, their relationships, their overall lives. My family, or any of the families in this book, could have been at risk had we lived in those times. I could have been one of those mothers.

I remember once walking towards the car with Tom after we had been to a therapy session, one he'd found particularly helpful and reassuring. He said to me, "I'm so lucky to have someone kind who can help me like that. I'm pleased I was born now and not 50 years ago." I wholeheartedly agreed with him, all too aware of how things may have played out in another era. Tom went on to ask, "What did people do before psychologists or doctors were around, before they knew about autism?" I replied that many people had a really hard time and were misunderstood. I didn't have the heart to tell him just how misunderstood. Thank goodness perceptions have shifted, and continue to do so.

Epilogue

The world has changed since I started writing this book—and never more dramatically than over the past few months. A pandemic is sweeping the globe and the outlook is frightening. It is a time of deep reflection for many people, and for me, it builds on some of the lessons I have learnt through the experience of being a parent and interviewing the people in this book. Personally, these are lessons around managing anxiety through letting go and being grateful. More universally, however, it highlights the notion that humanity is a diverse and complex collective—that we will all be exposed to illness or disability at some stage, and compassion is needed.

At the time of writing, Sydney is in lockdown. People are confined to their homes, banished from socialising, from seeing extended family and in many cases, from working. My giant teenage boys are home from school, spending endless hours on screens as they learn and play online. I can hear my neighbours making work calls in their backyard, or laughing or bickering. Our valuable community is now only available to us over the fence. Sometimes we bump into friends on the walking track and try to hide our excitement about the face-to-face contact, for everything else is behind a screen. I teach classes online; book club and drinks with the girls are online; my mother's 75th birthday is celebrated across three Australian states on Zoom. When is this going to end, we ask ourselves, each other, our television screens.

We learn to enjoy the simplicity of our new existence and acknowledge that this new way of life is not all bad. Chalk artworks and hopscotch squares appear on the footpath. Handmade mobiles swing from trees. The smell of brownies and sourdough spill from the kitchens of overflowing houses. I embrace the meditative value of obsessively piecing together a 1000 piece jigsaw puzzle of Bondi Beach with Otis, now 14, until midnight (and I am not normally a puzzle kind of person, finding them frustrating and time consuming). We know we should go to bed, but why, when we can wear our pyjamas to school or work the next morning? And when there is another puzzle piece of the Pacific Ocean to find, and another, and we can revel in the thrill of clicking it into place? Being in the moment becomes a survival tactic and reminds me of how I have managed other worrying times. Second guessing the future amid so much uncertainty is never going to help.

Tom, 16, is not much of a puzzle man, but his introvert tendencies have held him in good stead during lockdown. He misses rock-climbing, watching horror films with his friends and the newly discovered independence of travelling to the city by public transport. But online learning has been a boon. He is relaxed about doing his school work, and I am quietly amazed, as are his teachers. Able to work at his own pace without the distractions and stresses of a normal school day, his productivity has soared. It is wonderful to see him rewarded with accolades and being more self-directed than ever before. It certainly seems to be a style of learning that suits him.

Otis too has found his groove in this new world of isolation, navigating online learning and social distancing. He is understandably devastated that sports are cancelled, and even more so, that skateboard parks have closed. But with the luxury of time and a new cordless drill, he's built a skateboard box to use on the street. Like his brother, he's innovating and making the most of life in these unusual times. And I want to say that I've stopped worrying quite so much.

Who knows what the future will hold amid so much ambiguity? Of course, it is out of my control (anyone's control!) and I am again reminded of the importance of managing expectations. For now at least, I do my best at being present, while piecing together a huge jigsaw, whisky in hand. At first the puzzle is overwhelming and the little blue pieces all look the same. But over time, distinct shapes and hues materialize. Some pieces are cobalt and some are indigo, some form sky and some form ocean—each piece is precious and each plays a part in making up the whole intricate picture.

Author's note

When I first started this project in 2014, it was titled *Painting the spectrum: Everyday stories of families living with 'high functioning' autism*. I used the term 'high functioning' to show that I did not wish to speak for families who may be living with more severe forms of autism. I wanted to demonstrate that individuals who were so-called 'high functioning' had unique challenges, but could communicate and function in many areas of their life without assistance. This category could apply to children who attend mainstream schools or adults who live independently—and to individuals who were once diagnosed with Asperger's syndrome because of their normal to high IQ and communication abilities.

I have since found out, however, that the autism spectrum—much like life itself—does not work quite so conveniently. An autistic individual who does not communicate at age three may go on to speak extraordinarily well as an adult. A child who rattles off complete sentences at 18 months, may go on to have extreme difficulty with processing and learning as a teenager. A psychologist recently told me that the autism spectrum is not so much a continuum as a furry ball of wool. That is to say, the lived experiences of those on the spectrum resist well-ordered classification, and any classifications may be frayed at the edges. Indeed, I have found this to be true. I have also found that unravelling can come at the most unexpected of moments. That, of course, is not to diminish moments of warmth and sheer delight that I encountered when talking to the families featured in this book, and encounter every day when parenting my son.

At the time of writing, the diagnostic term 'high functioning' is not the preferred terminology in autism circles. Instead, individuals with autism are categorised into levels 1, 2 or 3, with 3 being the most debilitating. While useful, such categorisation can be political and may again change. We saw this in 2013 when Asperger's syndrome was removed from the Diagnosis and Statistical Manual of Mental Disorders (DSM-5) and merged in with Autism Spectrum Disorder (ASD).

I refer to Asperger's intermittently throughout this project, as this was the formal diagnosis received by many of the people I write about. Prior to 1994, the official diagnosis of Asperger's did not exist in Australia, or in the UK and US. Many individuals flew under the radar, struggled through, or in some cases were given incorrect and unhelpful diagnoses.

The term 'high functioning' autism is not ideal. I prefer 'on the spectrum' to reflect the scope of differences between individuals with autism, and I use this term throughout this project. The label 'high functioning' is not indicative of the debilitating challenges that some individuals experience and might inaccurately paint a picture of coping well with everyday tasks. The label 'low functioning' is similarly misleading and might be received as denigrating and disrespectful. It does not take into account an individual's ability and potential. Barry M. Prizant writes that such labels can predetermine how much support a child might receive: "if 'low', don't expect much' if 'high', she'll do fine and doesn't need support. The label often becomes a self-fulfilling prophecy."[85] I respect this view and have taken it into account when writing this project. I have chosen to put the words 'high functioning' inside inverted commas to indicate the distinction between the label and the actuality.

I am also mindful of other language around autism. In this project, I refer to people who are not on the spectrum as 'neurotypical' and might refer those who are, as 'neurodiverse', 'atypical' or 'differently wired'. I tend to use person-first language, for example 'a person with autism' rather than identity first language, for example 'autistic person'—although I do swap between the two. While some people believe that autism should not define them, others believe it is indeed integral to their identity. Artist Dawn Joy Leong, for example, told me that she prefers to be known as an 'autistic person' rather than an 'person with autism' because "autism is a neurological function not a disease or a handbag that one carries around."[86] She makes a great point and I honour this view. I have endeavoured to be as respectful as possible in my choice of words.

Acknowledgements

I am sincerely indebted to the families and individuals who allowed me into their homes and hearts, and who shared their stories with me. It is through your generosity that this book was made possible, and I thank you for your honesty, your time and for your tissues when needed.

Thank you to my patient husband 'James' who has remained encouraging and supportive throughout. Sorry it all took a little bit more time than expected, but we had some living to do. Thank you to my beautiful boys for keeping me grounded, and for allowing me to share our story in the hope that it will help others. To 'Tom', you are one amazing person and I'm so excited to see what pathway you will choose. To 'Otis', you are all kinds of awesome, a caring and wonderful person too. I love you all to bits.

This book was written as a part of a Doctorate of Creative Arts at Western Sydney University. I extend heartfelt thanks to my supervisor Dr Milissa Deitz and co-supervisor Dr Rachel Morley, who have not only provided scholarly guidance and support, but also friendship. Both are brilliant mentors and now colleagues.

I am also grateful to the Writing and Society Research Centre at the University, particularly Melinda Jewell; to the Varuna Writer's Centre, where I had two residencies, and to the wonderful writers I worked alongside there, including Louise Carter, Sarah Gilbert, Misty McPhail and Isabelle Li. Thanks also to Lynn Garlick for her camaraderie, and to Fiona Wright for encouraging me to write with vulnerability when we first met at Creative Ecologies. Thank you to Heather Grace Jones and Sally Treffry for kindly reading drafts, and for your insight and wisdom.

Love and thanks to Mum and Dad for always believing in me and for teaching me to have the courage of my convictions. To my mother-in-law, thank you for your support, and holding the fort so I could attend writing retreats and conferences. Cheers to my dear friends (you know who you are) for the fun, laughter and Prosecco.

Acknowledgements

Finally, thank you to all of the neurodiverse people who have taught me that while life may not be straight forward or predictable, it can be extraordinary.

Notes and references

Introduction

1   Goggin, G. & Newell, C. (2005). *Disability in Australia: Exposing a Social Apartheid.* Sydney: University of New South Wales Press Ltd. p. 28.
2   Sontag, S. (1991). *Illness as Metaphor and AIDS and its Metaphors.* New York: Farrar, Straus & Giroux.
3   On my extensive list of things to get done this remains high up, but not as yet quite high enough to actually get done!
4   At the time of writing, the NSW Government supported all of the recommendations (including increased funding) outlined in the Parliamentary Inquiry into 'Education of students with a disability or special needs in NSW', Parliament of NSW (2017).

Students with a Disability or Special Needs in New South Wales Schools. Retrieved from: https://www.parliament.nsw.gov.au/specialneedsstudents; Roy, D. (2018, February 8). NSW could lead the way in educating students with a disability. *The Conversation*. Retrieved from: https://theconversation.com/nsw-could-lead-the-way-in-educating-students-with-a-disability-80812; Roy, D. (2016, May 30). Children with disability are being excluded from education. *The Conversation*. Retrieved from: https://theconversation.com/children-with-disability-are-being-excluded-from-education-59825

5 Sutherland, K. (2017, October 23). Autism and the arts: making a space for different minds. *The Conversation*. Available: https://theconversation.com/autism-and-the-arts-making-a-space-for-different-minds-84768

6 The neurodiversity movement accepts diversity as playing an integral part in human evolution. It sees conditions such as autism, attention-deficit/hyperactivity disorder (ADHD) and dyslexia as "naturally occurring cognitive variations with distinctive strengths that have contributed to the evolution of technology and culture rather than mere checklists of deficits and dysfunctions" (Silberman, S., 2015, *Neurotribes: The Legacy of Autism and How to Think Smarter About People Who Think Differently*. Sydney: Allen & Unwin. p.16). Neurotypicals are people who do not present with these cognitive variations.

7   Sutherland, K. (2018, April 17). Employable Me has struck a chord but will it change employers' attitudes to disability?, *The Conversation*. Available: https://thecon versation.com/employable-me-has-struck-a-chord-but-will-it-change-employers-attitudes-to-disability-94903

Building blocks

8   Kirkland, A. (2012). Credibility battles in the autism litigation. *Social Studies of Science*. 42 (2), 237-261.
9   Donvan, J. & Zucker, C. (2016). *In a Different Key: The Story of Autism*. New York, NY: Crown Publishers.
10   Attwood, T. (2007). *The Complete Guide to Asperger's Syndrome*. London: Jessica Kingsley Publishers. p. 327.
11   Autism Spectrum Australia (2013). Retrieved from: https://www.autismspectrum.org.au/. Also note that 'high functioning' autism is now known simply as 'autism'.
12   cited in Solomon, A. (2014). *Far from the Tree: Parents, Children and the Search for Identity*, London: Vintage. p. 280.

Temples and towers

13   Greene, R. W. (1998). *The Explosive Child: A New Approach for Understanding and Parenting Easily Frustrated, "Chronically Inflexible" Children*. New York, NY: HarperCollins Publishers. p.325.

14   Young, S. (2014, April). I'm not your inspiration, thank you very much. TEDxSydney. [video file]. Retrieved from: https://www.ted.com/talks/stella_young _i_m_not_your_inspiration_thank_you_very_much

Same but different

15   Greene, R. W. (1998). p. 22-23.
16   ibid. p. 25.
17   Silberman, S. (2015) *Neurotribes: The Legacy of Autism and How to Think Smarter About People Who Think Differently*. Sydney: Allen & Unwin.
18   Elder Robison, J. (2016, September 11). *All in the Mind*, ABC Radio. Available from: http://www.abc .net.au/radionational/programs/allinthemind/tuning-in-to-autism/7819618
19   ibid.
20   Elder Robison, J. (2011). *Be Different: Adventures of a Free-range Aspergian*. North Sydney: Random House. p. 19.
21   ibid. pp. 24-25.

Secret garden

22   Homeschooling is becoming an increasingly popular way to educate students with ASDs. Homeschooling in NSW increased by 12% in 2016, compared to 1.1% in public school enrolments. Retrieved from: NSW Education Standards Authority. (2016). *Home*

Schooling Data Reports Relating to 2016. Retrieved from: http://educationstandards.nsw.edu.au. Of course, COVID-19 has seen many more children homeschooled through necessity.

23 Greene, R. W. (1998). p. 325.
24 French feminist cartoonist 'Emma' illustrates the concept of the mental load on this comic: https://www.theguardian.com/world/2017/may/26/gender-wars-household-chores-comic
25 Prizant, B. M. (2015). *Uniquely Human: A Different Way of Seeing Autism*. New York: Simon & Schuster. p.235.

Dolls in the closet

26 ibid. p. 54.
27 ibid. p. 57.
28 Attwood, T. (2007). *The Complete Guide to Asperger's Syndrome*. London: Jessica Kingsley Publishers. p. 199.
29 Asperger (1979) cited in Attwood (2007). p. 199.
30 cited in Yanofsky, J. (2012). *Bad animals: A Father's Accidental Education in Autism*. New York: Arcade Publishing. p. 141.
31 ibid. p. 142.
32 Lipscomb, M. & Stewart, A. (2014). Analysis of therapeutic gardens for children with autism spectrum disorders. *Perkins & Will Research Journal*, 6 (2). Retrieved: perkinswill.com/sites/default/files/ID%205_PWRJ_Vol0602_04_Analysis%20of%20Therapeutic%20Gardens.pdf

33 Silberman, S. (2015). p. 9.
34 Bickerton, A. & Nair. J. (2009). *Bowen meets Linehan*. Paper presented at the AN & NZ Family Therapy Conference, Sydney.

Through the looking glass

35 Prizant, B. M. (2015). p. 109.
36 Attwood, T. (2007); Kutscher, M.L. (2008). *ADHD: Living Without Brakes*. London: Jessica Kingsley Publishers.
37 Little (2002) cited in Attwood, T. (2007). p. 98.
38 Prizant, B. M. (2018, March 14) cited in *Tilt Parenting* [Audio podcast]. Available from: http://www.tiltparenting.com/2018/03/13/episode-99-barry-prizant-on-his-book-uniquely-human/
39 Dobbs, D. (2009, December). The science of success. *The Atlantic*. Retrieved from: https://www.theatlantic.com/magazine/archive/2009/12/the-science-of-success/307761/
40 Stroud, G. J. (2016, January). Teaching Australia. *Griffith Review*. Edition 51. Retrieved from: https://griffithreview.com/articles/teaching-australia/

Mushrooms and marjoram

41 Prizant, B. M. (2015). p. 4.
42 ibid. p. 5.
43 ibid. p. 187.
44 ibid. p. 4.

45   Grandin, T. & Moore, D. (2015). *The Loving Push: How Parents and Professionals Can Help Spectrum Kids Become Successful Adults*. Arlington, Tex: Future Horizons. p. vii.

46   ibid, p. xi.

The soprano

47   Kutscher, M.L. (2008).

48   Greene, R. W. (1998). p. 17.

49   ibid. p. 22.

50   cited in Attwood, T. (2007). p. 128.

51   ibid. p. 131.

52   Kutscher, M.L. (2008).

53   Prizant, B. M. (2015). p.120.

54   Attwood, T. (2007). p. 46. It should also be noted that while girls are less likely to be diagnosed that boys, they are "more vulnerable to internalising problems, such as anxiety, depression and eating disorders", hence the importance of further research in this area, timely diagnosis and support. Autism Awareness Australia (2020). 'Autism and girls'. Retrieved from https://www.autismawareness.com.au/could-it-be-autism/autism-and-girls/.

55   White, E. I., Wallace. G. L., Bascom, J., Armour, A. C., Register-Brown, K., Popal, H. S., Ratto, A. B., Martin, A. Kenworthy, L. (2017, October) Sex differences in parent-reported executive functioning and adaptive behavior in children and young adults with autism spectrum disorder. *Autism Research*.

(10), 10. pp. 1653-1662, Retrieved from: https://onlinelibrary.wiley.com/doi/abs/10.1002/aur.1811

Shifting perspectives

56   Silberman, S. (2015). p.15.
57   ibid. p. 17
58   Sontag, S. (1991).
59   Attwood, T. (2007). p. 327.
60   Churchman, F. & Saunders, T. (Presenters) (11 March 2019). Diagnosis [Audio podcast]. *The Parenting Spectrum*. Available from: https://www.abc .net.au/radio/programs/the-parenting-spectrum/
61   Dahl, M. (2016, October 18). A leading autism organization is no longer searching for a 'cure'. *The Cut*. Retrieved from: https://www.thecut.com/2016/10/autism-speaks-is-no-longer-searching-for-a-cure.html
62   Zablotsky, B., Bradshaw, C. P., Anderson, C. M., Law, L. (2013). Risk factors for bullying among children with autism spectrum disorders. *Autism*. (0) 0: 1-9. Retrieved from: http://citeseerx.ist.psu.edu/viewdoc/download?doi=10.1.1.922.5877&rep =rep1&type=pdf
63   First published in *The Conversation*. Sutherland, K. (2018, April 17).
64   Cohen, B. (2016). *Employable Me*. BBC Two. Series 1.
65   First published in *The Conversation*. Sutherland, K. (2017, April 28). Friday essay: moving autism on

TV beyond the genius stereotype, *The Conversation*. Available: https://theconversation.com/friday-essay-moving-autism-on-tv-beyond-the-genius-stereotype-76146

66   Silberman, S. (2015). p. 182.
67   Bolt, A. (2019, 1 August). The disturbing secret to the cult of Greta Thunberg. *The Herald Sun*. Retrieved from: https://www.heraldsun.com.au/blogs/andrew-bolt/the-disturbing-secret-to-the-cult-of-greta-thunberg/news-story/55822063e3589e02707fbb5a9a75d4cc
68   Bolt, A. (2019, 25 September). 'Filthy climate lies' are simply child abuse. *skynews.com.au*. Retrieved from: https://www.skynews.com.au/details/filthy-climate-lies-are-child-abuse-to-greta-turned-martyr
69   Donvan, J. & Zucker, C. (2016). *In a Different Key: The Story of Autism*. New York, NY: Crown Publishers. p. 91.
70   ibid. p. 93.
71   ibid. p. 88.
72   ibid. p. 192.
73   Silberman, S. (2015). p. 105.
74   Sheffer, E. (2018). *Asperger's Children: The Origins of Autism in Nazi Vienna*. New York: W. W. Norton & Company. p. 82
75   ibid. p. 90.
76   ibid. p. 248
77   Silberman, S. (2015). p. 138, 140.
78   ibid. p. 183.
79   ibid. p. 189.

80 ibid. p. 188-189.
81 ibid. p. 190.
82 ibid. p. 192.
83 This is highlighted in the book *Our House is on Fire: Scenes of a Family and a Planet in Crisis* (2020), an edited extract of which can be found here: https://www.theguardian.com/environment/2020/feb/23/great-thunberg-malena-ernman-our-house-is-on-fire-memoir-extract
84 Silberman, S. (2015). p. 288.

Author's note

85 Prizant, B. M. (2015). p. 221.
86 I interviewed Dawn Joy Leong for *The Conversation*. Sutherland, K. (2017, October 23).